Postcards
from
*Portugal

--- Memories and Recipes ---

Postcards from *Portugal

--- Memories and Recipes ---

PHOTOGRAPHY BY MANOS CHATZIKONSTANTIS
STYLING BY MICHAIL TOUROS
ART DIRECTION BY LISA GREENBERG
ILLUSTRATIONS BY MICHAIL TOUROS

Tessa Kiros

whitecap

This edition published in Canada in 2008 by Whitecap Books, 351 Lynn Ave.,
North Vancouver, British Columbia, Canada V7J 2C4.
www.whitecap.ca

First published by Murdoch Books Pty Limited in 2008.

Murdoch Books Pty Limited Australia
Pier 8/9, 23 Hickson Road, Millers Point NSW 2000
Phone: +61 (0)2 8220 2000 Fax: +61 (0)2 8220 2558
www.murdochbooks.com.au

Chief Executive: Juliet Rogers
Publisher: Kay Scarlett

Photography: Manos Chatzikonstantis
Styling and illustrations: Michail Touros
Art Direction: Lisa Greenberg
Editor: Jane Price
Designers: Sarah Odgers, Gayna Murphy
Food Editor: Michelle Earl
Production: Tiffany Johnson

ISBN 1-55285-889-8
ISBN 978-1-55285-889-9

Printed by 1010 Printing International Ltd in 2007. PRINTED IN HONG KONG.
Colour reproduction by Splitting Image Colour Studio, Melbourne, Australia.
First published 2008.

COOKING NOTES: You may find cooking times vary depending on the oven you are using. For fan-forced ovens, as a general
rule, set the oven temperature to 20°C (35°F) lower than indicated in the recipe. We have used 20 ml (4 teaspoon) tablespoon
measures. If you are using a 15 ml (3 teaspoon) tablespoon, for most recipes the difference will not be noticeable. However, for
recipes using baking powder, gelatine, bicarbonate of soda (baking soda) or small amounts of cornflour (cornstarch), add an
extra teaspoon for each tablespoon specified. We have used 59 g (2 oz) eggs.

- *Contents* -

I would have come here just for a *pastéis de nata*. Never mind the piri piri flattened chicken, grilled prawns, sardines and prego rolls. Oh, and for *azulejos*, wine and *fado*. But nobody told me about the bread. Or about the kindness of the Portuguese people.

My appreciation of Portuguese food started in South Africa, where it seeped through from Mozambique to the many restaurants and homes. Plus, all the greengrocers were Portuguese — a testimony to their love of the land. But mostly what intrigued me was the stretching out of Portugal to so many other and varied lands.

My travels took me through all of mainland Portugal and to the island of San Miguel in the Azores. I was charmed by the old-fashioned way of doing things in this ancient kingdom of Europe — so humble, unobtrusive and majestically beautiful. A land of many flowers and of charming homely tables laden with food marinated in spices picked from far-off lands. From the lands where the intrepid navigators once sailed in glorious caravels, through boiling oceans, past fabled monsters and battling with contrary winds and currents. Collecting spices to bring back to their cooking pots, they sowed seeds of their own spices and children in foreign lands and women. Exchanging between far-flung locales, pieces of language, gold, gems, recipes, architecture, porcelains and silks, they carried them right back to Belém on the banks of Lisbon's River Tejo. They brought a bit of the world — its people, religions and ideas — back to Portugal. And they accomplished all this largely with ships and men on the open oceans of the globe.

First to the Atlantic islands of Madeira, the Azores, and *Cabo Verde*, then down the west coast of Africa, around the Cape and into the Indian Ocean they sailed. By the time Vasco

For Mother Portugal, and everywhere she scattered her seeds

da Gama stepped from his ship in Calicut in 1498 and opened the spice route to India, the Portuguese seaborne enterprise was well on its way to becoming the dominant commercial empire of the day. In this golden age, the Portuguese colours were flying over many far-flung places on four continents.

This created a fascinating cross-pollination of people and places — *Cabo Verde*, Angola, Mozambique, São Tomé and Principe, Goa, Macau, Brazil, Guinea, the Azores, Madeira — that all go to make up the culture of Portugal past and present. This leads to surprise elements and ingredients in the food with interesting combinations: cinnamon and cloves, fresh coriander used in abundance, peppers, *feijoada*, coffee with steak, and, of course, the wonderful

piri piri. Many times I felt the Portuguese had been given a challenge — something similar to 'conundrum' where you have to find as many short words as you can from one long one. The Portuguese were given bacalhau and eggs to make as many things as they could. And so they went ahead… and invented a thousand recipes for bacalhau, and made all their desserts with egg.

Although the empire has faded, the result today is a land rich in the diversity of its people, food, art and respect for the faraway places it once dominated. And the soulful *fado* tunes are draped with the melancholy of splendid days gone by…

The Portuguese spirit AGUARDENTE (fire water) is used to marinate *ginja* (very similar to sour cherries) to make *ginjinha*, and splashed over savoury foods, such as chouriço, to flame and flavour. This strong, distilled sugarcane liqueur with its high alcohol content is also known as *cachaça* in Brazil. You can buy it under either name in most liquor stores, but if you have trouble finding it, you can use brandy or grappa instead.

I've included a recipe for a BREAD, but if you don't feel like making your own, use any dense-textured, country-style bread. As well as serving it with every meal, the Portuguese use their bread as an ingredient in dishes such as *açorda* and *migas*. For these recipes, use a loaf of day-old bread that is on the verge of staleness, rather than crumbly fresh.

The Portuguese have been enjoying BACALHAU (salt cod) since early in the sixteenth century when they had reached Newfoundland and started fishing the 'Grand Banks' for cod. It became so important to the Portuguese economy and such a staple for its people that it was given the nickname '*fiel amigo*', meaning faithful friend. Today there are said to be 365 different ways to prepare salt cod — one for every day of the year.

In many countries you can buy salt cod in the fishmongers, and in other countries you may have to go to a special supplier or Portuguese delicatessen. In some places you can buy it presoaked and ready to use, but often you'll need to soak it yourself to remove the excess salt that could spoil a meal. Rinse the cod pieces first, then put them in a large bowl with enough water to completely immerse them. Cover the bowl and refrigerate, changing the water 3–4 times a day. Ask your fishmonger how long you need to soak the cod (it's usually about 2–3 days). If you're unsure, test the cod by breaking off a small fleck, rinsing and tasting it. The tail part is always a bit more salty. If you're worried that it still smells too strong, even after soaking, try rinsing it in lemon juice. In some places you can buy convenient ready-soaked salt cod.

BAY leaves are widely used in Portuguese cooking. The flavour of the fresh leaves is intense and wonderful (if they crackle in the pan, just sit them on top of whatever else is cooking). If you're using dried leaves, don't keep them too long as they lose their intensity and flavour. If the recipe doesn't specify, then use fresh if you have them, otherwise dried are fine.

I adored the Portuguese abuse of COARSE SALT everywhere; it was one of the things I became most fond of. Coarse salt is not soft flakes of sea salt, but harder small crystals that don't dissolve as easily but crunch in the mouth. It is easily found in supermarkets and delicatessens. The Portuguese use coarse salt both as a seasoning (liberally), and for serving dishes such as eggs on salt.

CHOURIÇO is the most commonly found Portuguese sausage. These pork sausages, coloured by paprika and cooked over smoke, are both eaten on their own as a petisco plate, and as an ingredient in many dishes. If you can't find the Portuguese variety, Spanish chorizo is commonly available, or try Portuguese *linguiça* — a cooked smoked sausage that is thinner and less spicy. Sometimes the skin (casing) on chouriço can seem particularly thick and intrusive — if so, peel it away.

When a recipe calls for firm white FISH fillets, or a rounded whole fish, you could use any of the following: cod, sea bream (*pargo*), hake (*pescada*), halibut (*alabote*), haddock (*arnica*), cusk, whiting (*badejo*), snapper (*luciano*), seabass, swordfish (*espadarte*) or monkfish (*tamboril*). Flat fish include john dory (*galo*), flounder and sole. Good oily fish are trevally, mullet and mackerel (*carapau*). Other fish popularly used are tuna, salmon, skate (*raia*) and, of course, sardines.

PIRI PIRI is a hot chilli pepper, originally from Angola and embraced by the Portuguese who dribble piri piri oil over almost every dish. The chillies are red and slightly plump and known in some countries as bird's eye chillies, while the word 'piri piri' (or peri peri) tends to make us think of the fiery sauce which is readily available in supermarkets.

PIRI PIRI OIL

3–4 *medium-sized fresh* PIRI PIRI *chillies with seeds* (OR OTHER CHILLIES OF YOUR CHOICE) ·
6–8 *small dried* PIRI PIRI *chillies* · 1–2 GARLIC CLOVES, *peeled* · 2 TABLESPOONS WHISKY ·
½ TEASPOON *finely grated* LEMON ZEST * 1 TABLESPOON LEMON JUICE ·
1 TABLESPOON RED WINE VINEGAR · 1 BAY LEAF ·
1 TEASPOON COARSE SALT · 250 ML (9 FL OZ/1 CUP) OLIVE OIL

This is like a beautiful live fire. Use it here, use it there, use it just about anywhere if you love 'hot'. We have been drizzling it, very gently, onto lots of things. A drop onto your rice, into prego rolls, over a soup… even just a tiny drip will add a very different layer to your plate.

A good piri piri, Julio said, should burn only the outside of your mouth and not the inside. He knows this from a friend of his from Mozambique who gave him the recipe. 'Take any old bottle,' he said, 'rinse it and fill it about a third full with dried piri piri, crushed up or whole, however you like. You can splash with whisky, then cover with oil and leave to marinate. Just make sure it's completely covered by the oil so nothing goes mouldy.'

The heat of this will depend entirely on the potency of your chillies — I hope you can find piri piris for their flavour but, if not, use another variety of your choice.

Use an olive oil that's not too heavy or overpowering in its flavour. The heat will mellow with time, but once you have used up some of the oil, if you feel it's absolutely too strong, you can always top up with more oil.

Remove the green stems from the chillies and chop the chillies roughly. Pulse the chillies and garlic in a food processor or use a mortar and pestle to mash them to a paste. You need about 2 tablespoons of chilli paste.

Scrape out into a small saucepan, add the whisky and turn the heat to low. Add the lemon zest and juice, vinegar, bay and salt and about 2 or 3 tablespoons of the olive oil. (You can add some extra garlic if you feel you want it more garlicky.) Let it bubble up and 'roast' until it smells good. Remove from the heat and lightly whisk in the rest of the oil.

Pour into a sterilised jar and leave for a few days at least for the flavours to mingle. The oil will be hot at first but you'll find it will settle and mellow later and you can also sprinkle the crushed piri piris at the bottom over your food. You can add a stick or two of bay leaf twig to the oil if you like. *Makes about 325 ml (11 fl oz/1¼ cups)*

TOMATO PIRI PIRI SAUCE

250 ML (9 FL OZ/1 CUP) OLIVE OIL · 3 *RIPE* TOMATOES (100 G/3½ OZ EACH), *sliced* ·
50 G (1¾ OZ) BUTTER · A *generous* ½ TEASPOON SALT · A *large pinch of* SUGAR ·
6 DRIED PIRI PIRI CHILLIES, *or to taste, finely chopped (or pulsed in a processor)* ·
4 GARLIC CLOVES, *finely chopped (or pulsed in a processor)*

This is for serving with dishes like the grilled prawns, and is also lovely with the mixed fish grill. It's also used for mixing into the chicken livers (page 49) and is especially good just with grilled bread or over white rice. Once again, don't use an olive oil that is too strongly flavoured.

Heat the oil in a smallish heavy-based pan. Add the tomatoes and butter and simmer for about 25 minutes. Add the salt, sugar, piri piris and garlic and cook for another 5–10 minutes. Remove from the heat and purée roughly with a hand-held blender or food processor. If you like your sauce hotter, add a pinch or so of ground piri piri.

Pour into a sterilised jar, if you're not using immediately, and keep the surface covered with a layer of oil. Keep in the fridge and warm up or bring to room temperature to serve. This will keep for up to a month. *Makes about 435 ml (15 fl oz/1¾ cups)*

pimenta

AZOREAN RED PEPPERS

ABOUT 1 KG (2 LB 4 OZ) RED PEPPERS (_CAPSICUM_), _seeded and cut lengthways into quarters_ •
4 _heaped_ TABLESPOONS COARSE SALT • 3 FRESH BAY LEAVES • 3 GARLIC CLOVES, _unpeeled_

This is very typical in the Azores. It's often added to the pan after a steak or piece of tuna has been pan-fried. A rough paste (opposite) is also very popular and added as a seasoning to many dishes. The containers (ceramic or glass — no metal) you use must be cleaned and then sterilised with boiling water. Leave them to dry in a warm oven.

Lay each pepper quarter on your chopping board and crack down with your palm to flatten it completely. Start layering the peppers in a ceramic or glass container where they will fit compactly. After each layer of peppers, add a good sprinkling of salt, repeating until all the peppers and salt are used up.

Cover with plastic wrap and leave for 3 days or so (in the fridge in warm weather) until a brine has formed and the salt has dissolved. Shuffle the peppers once in a while to coat in the brine. Rinse the peppers under cold water and pat dry with kitchen paper.

Brush the peppers lightly with oil and then grill, skin side up, on a rack under a preheated hot grill. When the skins are charred and blistered, turn over and grill the other side for a few minutes. Leave to cool, then peel off the blackened skin.

When cold, pack into a sterilised jar, dotting the bay leaves and garlic cloves here and there between the layers. Cover completely with olive oil and keep in the fridge ready for use.

moida

MASSA DE PIMENTOS

— red pepper paste —

This can be used in a thousand ways. It's added to any stew for flavour, rubbed over meat before grilling, a dash can be thrown into the pot of white rice while it's cooking…

Shake out some of your peppers from the oil (see left — add a garlic clove from the oil, or a fresh one if you like) or purée some freshly chargrilled peppers with a little extra salt. Purée until as smooth as you can achieve, adding a few drops of water to move it along if it gets stuck. It will probably be quite a rough purée and still have some chunks. Scrape into a bowl and measure out roughly. For each $1/4$ cup of pepper purée, stir in (don't purée) a tablespoon of olive oil, a teaspoon of lemon juice and a few drops of vinegar. Put in a jar, cover with a layer of oil and keep in the fridge ready for use.

– First impressions –

I love this land and its people, covered in lace and church and simplicity,
in majestic mystery and understated honesty. Asleep, yet deep. Something regal.
Something sad. Superstitious, unrehearsed and humble, extremely helpful are the
people. The beautiful, deep, grey-blue Atlantic water (with not many swimmers
because of its ice-coldness) results in a totally un-European summer atmosphere,
as if something has stopped in time. And the prego rolls and *bifanas* are just right.
Soft, warm rolls with juicy meat inside. People with faded turquoise picnic
hampers flock under the pines, generations mingling unnoticed. Even the
highway stops are nice. Sandwiches packed by human hands for humans. You can
see that mass tourism and mass advantage-taking hasn't arrived in these parts.
I am impressed with the Portuguese.
We turn up the steep road to the *pousada* where we are staying in the north, past
the ladies making churros, the men selling compact discs and up the cobbled,
uneven, deep-grey street with its purply flowers.

pão

BREAD AND BREAD ROLLS
— the making of —

STARTER: 25 G (1 OZ) FRESH YEAST OR 15 G (¹⁄₂ OZ) DRIED YEAST ·
250 ML (9 FL OZ/1 CUP) *warm* WATER · 200 G (7 OZ) BREAD FLOUR · A *pinch of* SUGAR

450 G (1 LB) BREAD FLOUR · 50 G (1³⁄₄ OZ) RYE FLOUR · 1 *heaped* TEASPOON FINE SALT ·
1 TABLESPOON OLIVE OIL · 200 ML (7 FL OZ) *warm* WATER

This is a lovely bread that reminds me of Portugal and the rolls are great for 'pregos'. Use oat flour instead of rye if you like, or change the proportions for a different flavour.

To make the starter, whisk everything together in a largish bowl (roomy enough for the dough to double in size) until you have a smooth thick batter. Cover with plastic wrap and leave in a warm place for a few hours until puffed. (If you like, you can then refrigerate for 2–3 days, but take it out of the fridge and bring back to room temperature a couple of hours before using.)

Mix in the remaining ingredients, mixing very well even though it may seem a bit sticky.

If you have a mixer with a dough hook this is quick and easy to do.

Tip out onto a lightly floured work surface and gently knead, turning the bread around over itself (I worked it for about 10–15 minutes). You won't need to add any extra flour for kneading here. Put in a large bowl, cover with a heavy tea towel and leave in a fairly warm place for 2–3 hours until it has risen right up and is nice and puffed.

Take out the dough, trying not to punch it right down but gently easing it into an oval or circle. Slash the top and put on a baking tray dusted with flour. Cover loosely with a tea towel and leave to rise again for another hour while you preheat the oven to 220°C (425°F/Gas 7).

Put in the oven and flick a bit of water here and there on the bread to give it a good crispy crust. Bake for 40–45 minutes until crusty and the loaf sounds hollow when you tap it on the base. Leave to cool on a rack. This gives a gorgeous big loaf — I always cut it into quarters and freeze two of them.

BREAD ROLLS: After the final rising, divide the dough into 12 portions and roll out on your work surface into balls, then smooth and flatten a bit into thickish ovals about 10 cm (4 inches) across. Cut a slash down the middle of each one with the back of a dinner knife (or use the round handle of a wooden spoon), cutting almost all the way through but not quite. Twist and roll the ends out into points and then put on two baking trays dusted with flour. Dust lightly with flour (I put some flour in a sieve), cover with a tea towel and leave for another hour to puff up while you preheat your oven to 180°C (350°F/Gas 4).

Before you put them in the oven, gently remake the slashes that may have puffed up, taking care not to deflate the rolls. Bake for about 20 minutes until the rolls are pale golden and sound hollow when you tap them on the base. They will not be too crusty. Cool on a rack first, then shake off any excess flour. They should be just lightly dusted (if they look as if they need a bit more flour, turn them upside down and dip them in the cooked flour on the baking tray).

The Thursday market in northern Barcelos is an understated beauty. Squawking chickens mixed in back to back with fresh fruit and flowers, seeds, olives and lupini all in lovely coloured plastic bowls. Imperfect packaging, different to elsewhere and very alive. On the way back, bacalhau displayed in a shop together with clocks and religious icons. Mixed in with some gypsy-looking floral scarves and a language from nowhere I know. And yet, even among the noise and chaos, there is a certain Portuguese stillness.

nova vaga
CABELEIREIRAS

nova vaga
CABELEIREIRAS

PORTO

- *Petisco Plates* -

SMALL BITES

CORREIO
DE
PORTUGAL

SELOS

to start...

TUNA OR SARDINE PATE

TUNA: 100 G (3½ OZ) *unsalted* BUTTER · 100 G (3½ OZ) TIN *best-quality* TUNA *IN OIL*, DRAINED ·
2 ANCHOVIES *IN OIL, drained* · A SPLASH OF LEMON JUICE · *a pinch of* GROUND PIRI PIRI

SARDINE: 100 G (3½ OZ) *unsalted* BUTTER · 1 TEASPOON TOMATO PASTE ·
120 G (4½ OZ) TIN *PORTUGUESE* SARDINES IN OIL, *drained* · *a splash of* WHISKY ·
a pinch of GROUND PIRI PIRI · SOME *chopped* PARSLEY, *IF YOU LIKE*

Tuna or sardine paté comes before every meal in Portugal, it seems. It is on the table as soon as you sit down, in tiny pre-packed butter-like parcels, to be spread over some lovely bread. You can add whatever flavourings you might like here... some more lemon, chopped parsley or any other herb. Make sure the butter and fish are well puréed for no lumps. Depending on the butter and anchovies you use, you might not need any extra salt.

TUNA: Use a hand-held blender or pulse the butter, tuna and anchovies in a food processor to blend. Sprinkle in the lemon juice, piri piri, some pepper, salt if needed, and blend again.

Cover and refrigerate for up to a few days if you are not serving immediately (but take it out of the fridge well before you serve, so that it's not rock hard). This is lovely spread on warm toast. *Makes about 200 g (7 oz/1 cup)*

SARDINE: Use a hand-held blender or pulse the butter, tomato paste and sardines in a food processor to blend well. Sprinkle in the whisky, piri piri, pepper and a little salt, if you like, and blend until smooth. Fold in the parsley.

Cover and refrigerate for up to a few days if you are not serving immediately (but take it out of the fridge well before you do serve, so that it's not rock hard). *Makes about 200 g (7 oz/1 cup)*

lupini

OLIVES, CHOURICO, LUPINI BEANS AND EGGS

MARINATED OLIVES: 200 G (7 OZ) *BLACK OR GREEN* OLIVES *in brine* · 4 TABLESPOONS OLIVE OIL ·
2 TABLESPOONS RED WINE · 2 TEASPOONS RED WINE VINEGAR ·
1 *LARGE* GARLIC CLOVE, *peeled and halved lengthways* · A *sprinkling of* DRIED OREGANO FLOWERS ·
3–4 *SMALL* OLIVE LEAVES · COARSE SALT

1 CHOURICO *sausage* · AGUARDENTE *or brandy* · LEMONS · LUPINI BEANS · EGGS

 These are a few things that are served regularly on the petisco plate before the main meal in Portugal.

MARINATED OLIVES: You can make as many or as few of these as you like. I love the small olive leaves in here, and the colour the garlic takes on — they look beautiful. Use the leaves from a bonsai olive tree or just the smallest leaves from a regular olive tree.

You can choose olives already in brine (not a marinade), then rinse them well, even in warm water for a moment, and drain. If you're using salted olives, they should also be rinsed

and drained. Once your olives are eaten you can add some more to the marinade, or splash the leftover marinade over salad or bread.

Prick the rinsed olives with a toothpick. Put them in a bowl and mix with the oil, red wine, vinegar, garlic, oregano flowers and olive leaves. Scatter with coarse salt and pepper.

Cover and leave to marinate for a few days to infuse the flavours before serving.

GRILLED CHOURICO: In Portugal I would often see special terracotta chouriço-grillers, boat-shaped and with their terracotta racks on top, like the one in the photograph. The chouriço is put on the top rack and flamed with aguardente (a Portuguese spirit) which is splashed onto the bottom of the dish under the rack. The chouriço is cooked until it is crusty here and there. You could also cook this on a chargrill pan or the barbecue grill and serve as an appetiser while you have some other things going on for a main course.

Slash the chouriço here and there on top and put it on the chouriço-griller, chargrill pan or barbecue grill. Light up your griller or heat up the pan or grill. Cook and turn the sausage for a few minutes over high heat until it's hot and gets nice and crusty. Splash on a little more aguardente or brandy and let the flames whoosh up. The alcohol burns away while the chouriço cooks on the direct flame. Serve hot with great crusty bread and a lemon wedge or two.

LUPINI BEANS: These are quite lovely dusty yellow beans, a bit like broad beans, that are prepared in a brine. They are everywhere in Portugal, and nibbling on them is a lovely way to pass your time as you sit on a bar stool. In the *cervejaria* they are served with drinks as part of a petisco plate alongside olives, chouriço and more. You need to bite the tip off one end and then squeeze out the bean firmly from its outer jacket with your thumb and forefinger and pop it into your mouth. On every bar there were just piles of lupini skins on small plates and everyone with a beer or glass of wine. At the markets there are beautiful buckets of them everywhere. Everyone eats lupini. You can pick up some lupini beans in their brine from a specialist deli that stocks Portuguese products. They come in see-through vacuum-packed packets or large jars. All you need to do is soak them in cold water for an hour or so. Taste to check that they are not still briny, then drain and serve.

EGGS ON SALT: I loved the way, in some bars, the hard-boiled eggs sit on a plate scattered with coarse salt.

Put 6 room-temperature eggs in a large saucepan of cold water and bring slowly to the boil. As they come to the boil give them a stir for a couple of minutes so that the yolks are centred. Boil for 8 minutes, then drain and cool under cold water. You can leave them unpeeled and sit them on some salt so they don't roll, or peel them straightaway and serve with a little hill of coarse salt for scattering.

chouriço

BROAD BEANS WITH CHOURICO

500 G (1 LB 2 OZ) *shelled* FRESH (OR FROZEN) BROAD BEANS (*about 3 kg/6 lb 12 oz in their pods*) ·
2 TABLESPOONS OLIVE OIL · 160 G (5¾ OZ) CHOURICO SAUSAGE, *chopped* ·
1 SMALL RED ONION, *chopped* · 2 GARLIC CLOVES, *chopped* · 125 ML (4 FL OZ/½ CUP) WHITE WINE ·
6–8 MINT OR CORIANDER (*CILANTRO*) LEAVES, *torn* · A *splash of* RED WINE VINEGAR

This is lovely to make in the short season when we can get fresh broad beans. It can be quite a job on account of peeling the beans, but also rather relaxing. I like to peel away the outer jacket of each par-boiled bean, even if it makes for extra work. The insides are a beautiful, brighter green and are added to the pan towards the end of the cooking so they keep their colour.

Rinse the shelled beans and put them (or the frozen beans) in a pan of lightly salted boiling water and boil for about 5 minutes. Drain and peel off the outer skins. Many of them will split in half but that's fine — they are still lovely and smooth and beautiful.

Heat the oil in a large non-stick frying pan and sauté the sausage slices for a couple of minutes. Add the onion and cook, stirring, for a few more minutes until it is sticky and the sausage is brown.

Add the garlic and stir until you start to smell it, then add the wine and a couple of twists of pepper. Cook until the wine has evaporated a bit, then stir in the broad beans and cook for a couple of minutes over high heat so the flavours will mingle. There should be just a bit of sauce in the bottom of the pan. Stir in the mint or coriander at the end and a splash of red wine vinegar. Check for seasoning and serve warm with grilled bread or just-boiled potatoes. *Serves 4–6*

CHOURICO WITH
GREEN PEPPERS AND PORT

2 TABLESPOONS OLIVE OIL · 85 G (3 OZ) CHOURICO SAUSAGE, *roughly chopped* ·
1 GREEN PEPPER (*CAPSICUM*), *seeded and roughly chopped* · 1 SMALL ONION, *roughly chopped* ·
2 GARLIC CLOVES, *chopped* · 1 BAY LEAF · A *SPLASH OF* RUBY PORT

Make this the meal instead of a petisco, if you like, by serving it with a big salad, sautéed potatoes or a hunk of bread, a wedge of cheese and maybe a spoonful of quince marmalade.

Heat the oil in a large frying pan and cook the chouriço, green pepper and onion over medium heat until the onion is well browned and sticky looking and the pepper still has some crunch. Add the garlic and bay leaf and cook for a few more minutes until all is golden and crusty.

Splash in about 2 tablespoons of port and let that bubble up and evaporate until it all looks a bit sticky and shiny. Your chouriço should provide enough seasoning here, but taste at the end and add salt and pepper if you think it needs it. *Serves 2*

- *We arrive in the capital* -

Yesterday we left the north behind and drove towards Fatima.
We dropped our prayers with the dripping candle wax into the allocated space —
one for the world, one for us — and off we went again, away from the people
crawling up the path of promises. A place of special somethings, however you look
at it. And on we drove to Lisbon. I had been hoping for those pastel-coloured
water-reflecting buildings, but I saw none. It seemed an average-looking place.
But we were tired. So we unpacked. (I never felt good in any place, I found, until
I had walked at least twice on its stones.)
I woke this morning to find I love Lisbon. We have wonderful sardines *in escabeche*
(and I give you the very recipe) and bacalhau in many ways. On the walls of the
hotel are painted crests of all Portugal's colonies past and present: Madeira, the
Azores, São Tomé and Principe, Mozambique, Angola, Goa…
With every meal comes beautiful bread — a heavy, airy, chewy bread. Sometimes
white, sometimes a taupy colour, or white rolls, floury on the outside. And I love
the little packets of sardine and tuna paté that come with it. The streets are
slippery with beautiful stones and hills wander up and down in no apparent
direction, and I do wonder how people don't slip on them. Maybe it is my shoes.
Lisbon is exciting and a surprise and the *fado* makes me nostalgic.

sardinhas

SARDINES IN ESCABECHE

6–8 SARDINES (*about* 250 G/9 OZ), *cleaned and gutted* · CORNFLOUR (*CORNSTARCH*) ·
OLIVE OIL, *for frying* · 1 SMALL ONION, *sliced into rings* · 1 CARROT, *peeled and thinly sliced on the diagonal* ·
1 GARLIC CLOVE, *chopped* · 1 TEASPOON TOMATO PASTE ·
125 ML (4 FL OZ/½ CUP) WHITE WINE VINEGAR · 1 TABLESPOON RUBY PORT ·
1 TABLESPOON *chopped* PARSLEY

These are quick to make and keep well in the fridge for a day or so. The Portuguese will often use smaller sardines for a dish like this, while the larger plumper catch are saved for the charcoal grill. These are lovely with bread at room temperature, or even cold when they've been sitting for a while and have soaked up the flavours. If you prefer, you can fillet the fish first (it's not such a hectic job), so you don't have to fiddle with the bones on your plate.

Rinse the sardines and pat dry. Pat well in the cornflour to coat on both sides. Heat the oil in a small non-stick frying pan that will hold the sardines in a single layer without being too tightly packed. Fry the fish until deep gold and crusty on both sides. Drain on kitchen paper and put into a dish where they fit snugly in a single layer.

Heat 2 tablespoons of olive oil in a small pan and sauté the onion for a minute or so. Add the carrot and cook until just slightly softened. Add the garlic and, when you start to smell it, add the tomato paste. Stir well, then add the vinegar and port. Bubble up for 5 minutes or so until it thickens, add 125 ml (4 fl oz/½ cup) of water and carry on cooking for another few minutes until you have a good sauce.

Pour over the fried sardines so that they are covered, then scatter with some coarse salt and pepper. Sprinkle with the parsley just before serving, either warm or cold. *Serves 2–3*

camarão

PRAWN PASTRIES

PASTRY: 150 ML (5 FL OZ) MILK · ½ TEASPOON SALT · 50 G (1¾ OZ) BUTTER ·
250 G (9 OZ/2 CUPS) PLAIN (*ALL-PURPOSE*) FLOUR

FILLING: 180 G (6½ OZ) RAW PRAWNS *with shells but no heads* · 1 BAY LEAF ·
125 ML (4 FL OZ/½ CUP) MILK · 50 G (1¾ OZ) BUTTER · 1 SHALLOT, *finely chopped* ·
1 *SMALL* CELERY STALK, *finely chopped* · 2 TABLESPOONS *chopped* PARSLEY ·
A *good pinch of* GROUND PIRI PIRI · ¼ TEASPOON PAPRIKA · 1 GARLIC CLOVE, *chopped* ·
2 TEASPOONS TOMATO PASTE · 2 TABLESPOONS PLAIN (*ALL-PURPOSE*) FLOUR ·
grated zest and juice from HALF A SMALL LEMON

1 LARGE EGG, *lightly beaten* · ABOUT 3 CUPFULS OF BREADCRUMBS, *to coat* ·
OLIVE OIL, *for frying* · LEMON WEDGES, *to serve*

This might seem a touch long and fiddly, but you could break up the workload: make the prawn filling and pastry in the morning, keep it in the fridge, bring back to room temperature, then roll and refrigerate and fry the pastries before dinner, say. These are really wonderful as an appetiser before a seafood meal, or as a simple lunch with a big green salad. You could also add a grating or two of fresh nutmeg in place of the paprika and some coriander or other herbs instead of the parsley.

Fresh breadcrumbs are best for coating: just pulse two- or three-day old country-style bread in a food processor. You can keep these in the freezer and top them up whenever you have leftover bread.

To make the pastry, put the milk, salt, butter and 150 ml (5 fl oz) of water in a smallish heavy-based pan and bring to the boil. Just as it starts to come to the boil, take the pan off the heat and pour in the flour all in one go. Stir with a wooden spoon, then put it back on the heat, mixing until it all comes together in a ball. Leave to cool.

Make the filling. Simmer the prawns and bay leaf in the milk mixed with 125 ml (4 fl oz/ 1/2 cup) of water for 5 minutes or so until just cooked but still tender. Remove from the heat and drain, keeping the liquid. Peel the prawns, discarding the shells, and roughly chop.

Heat the butter in a small non-stick frying pan and sauté the shallot. When it starts to turn golden, add the celery and sauté until that too is golden, then add the parsley, piri piri, paprika and garlic. When you start to smell the garlic, add the tomato paste. Cook for a moment, then stir in the flour and finally add all the prawn cooking liquid. Boil up, then reduce the heat and simmer for 5 minutes or so until thickened. Remove from the heat, stir in the prawns, lemon zest and juice and season with salt and pepper. Leave to cool slightly.

Lightly dust your work surface with flour. Pat your hands in flour and pat the top of the pastry too. Roll out to about 2 mm (1/16 inch) thick (you might find it easier to roll the pastry in two lots). Cut out 10 cm (4 inch) circles with a pastry cutter and dollop a heaped teaspoon of

filling in the middle of each one. Dip your finger in water and run it along the edge of the pastry. Turn over and push down on the edge firmly to seal. Keep rolling out the scraps of pastry — you should get about 20 parcels.

Whip the egg with some salt and pepper in a flattish bowl. Put the breadcrumbs onto a plate. Pour enough oil into a large frying pan to come about halfway up the pastries when they're frying, and line a plate with kitchen paper ready for draining them.

Dip the well-sealed pastries in the egg, turning to coat both sides. Pat in breadcrumbs on both sides while your oil is heating (not too hot, or they'll burn before they cook through), then put the pastries in the pan — as many as will fit in a single layer. Fry until the undersides are beautifully golden, then turn them over with tongs or an egg slice, taking care not to pierce them. Fry until golden and crisp, then drain on kitchen paper while you fry the rest. Eat warm with lemon juice and salt.

The pastries can also be frozen before dipping in egg and breadcrumbs. Freeze them on a tray, crack them off and put them into a container flash frozen.

Makes about 20

Chaves

CHOURICO CAKE

5 EGGS · 100 G (3½ OZ/½ CUP) *melted and cooled* BUTTER · 5 TABLESPOONS OLIVE OIL ·
185 ML (6 FL OZ/¾ CUP) MILK · 310 G (11 OZ/2½ CUPS) CAKE *(00)* OR PLAIN *(ALL-PURPOSE)* FLOUR ·
2 TEASPOONS BAKING POWDER · ½ TEASPOON SALT · 100 G (3½ OZ) PRESUNTO, PROSCIUTTO *or*
similar HAM, *in one thickish slice* · 100 G (3½ OZ) CHOURICO SAUSAGE

This is Maria Alice's recipe from Chaves, the place she comes from right up in the north of Portugal. It's almost a bread; in fact, you can bake it in a loaf tin if you like. Serve it as you would a bread with a meal, or on its own as a snack any time you feel like something salty. I like the hint of chouriço that comes shining through just after you've taken a bite, but if you want it stronger then just add more.

Heat the oven to 200°C (400°F/Gas 6). Butter and flour a large ring tin (the sort you'd make a crème caramel in).

Beat the eggs with electric beaters until very fluffy and creamy. Add the butter and oil, whisking in well. Add the milk and flour in alternate batches, mixing the baking powder and salt into the flour. Whisk until you get a smooth batter.

Chop up the ham and chouriço, crumbling it through your fingers to separate any pieces that are stuck together, and stir into the mixture. Scrape into the tin and bake for 35 minutes or so until puffed and golden (if you're using a loaf tin, cook it for 5 minutes longer). Cool a little, remove from the tin and then slice into thick chunks to serve. *Serves 8–10*

GRATINEED MUSSELS

ABOUT 35 *LARGE-ISH* MUSSELS · 3 GARLIC CLOVES, *peeled, 1 left whole and 2 finely chopped* ·
2-3 TABLESPOONS WHITE WINE · 2 PARSLEY SPRIGS · 1 TABLESPOON OLIVE OIL ·
1 SHALLOT, *finely chopped* · JUICE *OF HALF A* LEMON · 2 HEAPED TABLESPOONS *chopped* PARSLEY ·
A good pinch of GROUND PIRI PIRI · BREADCRUMBS, *for sprinkling*

This is Daniela's recipe. She is Portuguese and was born in Mozambique, and her parents now live in Lisbon. She's a wonderful cook and these, I think, are fabulous to precede any seafood meal. Before you start cooking your mussels you need to 'de-beard' them by pulling away those fiddly bits of algae that stick out. Cut them off with scissors or a knife if you can't detach them, then scrub the shells well with a wire brush to dislodge evidence of the sea. At this stage you need to discard any mussels that are open and don't close when you give them a tap.

Fresh breadcrumbs are best for sprinkling over the top: just pulse two- or three-day old country-style bread in a food processor. You can keep these in the freezer and top them up whenever you have leftover bread.

⤳

Put your cleaned mussels into a pot, add the whole garlic clove, a couple of splashes of white wine, the parsley, some salt and pepper. Turn the heat to high, cover the pot and steam for about 3 minutes, or until the mussels open (discard any that remain stubbornly closed). Leave to cool. (You don't need the liquid here, but it's nice to

stir into some simmering rice to serve later.) You can steam the mussels beforehand if it's helpful, and leave to cool with the lid on.

Preheat the oven to 200°C (400°F/ Gas 6). Pick the mussels out of the shells and save the shell halves — you won't use all the shells (you'll need about 24), so pick out the best clean sides without the point at which the mussel was attached, and save some extra just in case. Put the shell halves in a single layer in a dish that can go from oven to table.

Chop the mussel meat finely. Heat the olive oil in a small pan and sauté the shallot until golden. Add the chopped garlic and stir until you start to smell it. Add the mussel meat, lemon juice, parsley, piri piri and some salt and pepper. Cook for just a moment once you've added the mussels, then turn off the heat when it is still a bit liquidy.

Spoon a teaspoonful into each shell so they are not too tightly packed. Sprinkle lightly with breadcrumbs and gratinée in the oven for 10 minutes, or until a bit golden but not dried out. Serve straight from the oven, or at room temperature. *Makes 24*

PRAWNS WITH PIRI PIRI, WHISKY AND LEMON

400 G (14 OZ) RAW PRAWNS · 1 TABLESPOON OLIVE OIL · 50 G (1³/₄ OZ) BUTTER · 2 SMALL BAY LEAVES · 2 GARLIC CLOVES, *chopped* · 1 TABLESPOON *chopped* PARSLEY · GROUND PIRI PIRI · ¹/₂ TEASPOON SWEET PAPRIKA · 3-4 TABLESPOONS WHISKY · *juice of* 1 SMALL LEMON · *extra* LEMONS, *to serve*

Tavira is a wonderfully sleepy, ancient town in Portugal's south. I ate this one night in a small restaurant there and it was so lovely that I asked the lady how she made it. This makes a perfect starter before a main course of grilled fish.

Remove the heads from the prawns but leave the shells on the bodies. Make a shallow cut down the back of each one so they take in the flavour of the sauce and devein them. Rinse and pat dry.

Heat the oil and half the butter in a large non-stick saucepan until very hot and sizzling. Throw in the prawns and bay leaves gradually, trying not to lose the heat, so the prawns get crusty and golden. Toss the pan and season with coarse salt and pepper. When the prawns are nicely golden on both sides, add the garlic, parsley, as much piri piri as you like, the paprika and the last of the butter.

Toss until you can smell the garlic, then add the whisky. When it's been absorbed, add the lemon juice and toss it all together. Let it bubble up for a moment, check the seasoning, then use a slotted spoon to lift the prawns onto a plate.

Add about 4 tablespoons of water to the pan and let it bubble up to thicken the sauce. Remove from the heat, return the prawns to the pan and toss through the sauce. Serve with some bread for the sauce and a lemon wedge or two. *Serves 3–4*

bacalhau

SALT COD AND CHICKPEAS

400 G (14 OZ) DRIED CHICKPEAS · A *few slices of* ONION ·
A *few small pieces each of* CARROT AND CELERY · 1 BAY LEAF ·
1 *small* WHITE OR RED ONION, *sliced into thin rings* · 1 TABLESPOON RED WINE VINEGAR ·
½ TEASPOON SALT · 250 G (9 OZ) BACALHAU (SALT COD), *soaked* · 2 TABLESPOONS *chopped* PARSLEY ·
A *handful of any* BLACK OLIVES *that you love*, PITTED · A *pinch of* PAPRIKA, *to serve*

DRESSING: 125 ML (4 FL OZ/½ CUP) OLIVE OIL · 2 TABLESPOONS RED WINE VINEGAR ·
JUICE *of half a* LEMON · A *pinch of ground* PIRI PIRI ·
ABOUT ½ TEASPOON *GROUND SWEET* PAPRIKA · 1 GARLIC CLOVE, *mashed*

This I ate in Ponte de Lima, made by the lovely old lady with her coloured shawl and long dangly gold earrings. She had a way of cutting all her vegetables that might have suggested a shaky hand, an aged, patient hand that had been doing this for ever so long. You can add whatever you like to these: some fresh coriander or chopped-up roasted peppers would be lovely, and I love hard-boiled and halved eggs here, or anything else that strikes you as good. This can be made beforehand, leaving it to marinate. Just pull it out of the fridge to add to your table at the very last moment.

Before you use the salt cod you need to soak it to remove the excess salt. Rinse the cod pieces first, then put them in a large bowl with enough water to completely immerse them. Cover the bowl and refrigerate, changing the water several times a day. Ask your fishmonger how long you need to soak the cod (it's usually 2–3 days). If you're unsure, test the cod by breaking off a small fleck, rinsing and tasting it. The tail part is always a bit more salty. In some places you can buy ready-soaked salt cod which is very reliable and convenient.

Put the chickpeas in a large bowl, cover with cold water and leave to soak for 8 hours or overnight. Drain and rinse the chickpeas and put in a pan with a slice or two of the onion, a piece each of carrot and celery and the bay leaf. Cover with water and bring to the boil. Skim the surface and simmer for 40 minutes until tender. Salt at the end of cooking and drain away the water, discarding the onion, carrot, celery and bay leaf.

Put the onion rings in a small bowl and cover with cold water. Add the vinegar and salt. Leave for 30 minutes or so and then drain.

Meanwhile, bring a small pan of water to the boil with the remaining onion, carrot and celery. Drain your bacalhau and add to the pan. Bring back to the boil and cook for 5 minutes

or so until cooked (taste a little flake of fish to check it's not still too salty: if it is, change the water and boil for a few more minutes). Drain away the water and leave the bacalhau to cool, then tear it into chunks, as small or large as you like, discarding all the skin and checking carefully for bones.

Make a dressing by whisking together the olive oil, vinegar, lemon juice, piri piri, paprika and garlic.

Put the chickpeas, bacalhau, onion, parsley and olives into a large serving bowl and pour the dressing over the top. Mix through well, adding salt if necessary and pepper to suit your tastes. Sprinkle with a dash of paprika to serve. *Serves 4–6*

I set off for Belém, through Baixa, up and down about seven hills, until the river came into view and then I knew to turn right. Into the food market for a quick peep – past more beautiful tiles, then neat piles of eggs, lovely huge pale oval melons and bay leaves fresh and drying everywhere, with some restrained cabbages and greens amongst a bit of tinsel and some Portuguese flags for the football that had just been. (I had noticed Portugal playing Angola, their former colony, and both teams talking, of course, in Portuguese.)

CHICKEN GIBLETS A PORTUGUESA

4 TABLESPOONS OLIVE OIL · 1 ONION, *chopped* ·
600 G (1 LB 5 OZ) CHICKEN GIBLETS OR LIVERS, *trimmed, cleaned and halved if large* · 2 BAY LEAVES ·
2-3 GARLIC CLOVES, *finely chopped* · 1½ TEASPOONS GROUND CUMIN · A *pinch of ground* PIRI PIRI ·
2 *LARGE RIPE* TOMATOES, *peeled and chopped or grated* · 125 ML (4 FL OZ/½ CUP) WHITE WINE

This is from Natasha's aunt, Helen. If you can't find chicken giblets you can make this with livers — it is just as nice. I particularly like the flavour of the cumin in here.

Heat the oil in a large frying pan and cook the onion until golden, then add the giblets or livers and brown them well.

Add the bay leaves, garlic, cumin, piri piri and season with salt and pepper. Once you start to smell the garlic, add the tomato. Cook until it's all turning jammy and the giblets are tender, then add the wine. Cook for about 10 minutes if you're using livers, or about 15–20 minutes for the giblets, until you have a lovely thick sauce (you may need to add a bit more wine or water once it's bubbling). Serve hot — it's lovely mashed up onto thick slices of bread. *Serves 4*

hot hot

PIRI PIRI CHICKEN LIVERS

250 ML (9 FL OZ/1 CUP) TOMATO PIRI PIRI SAUCE *(page 15)* · 30 G (1 OZ) BUTTER ·
1 TEASPOON *DRIED* OREGANO LEAVES · 600 G (1 LB 5 OZ) *cleaned* CHICKEN LIVERS, *halved or smaller* ·
JUICE OF 1 LEMON · *A small sprinkling of ground* PIRI PIRI, *IF YOU LIKE*

My friend, Corinne, taught me these — she used to make them in her restaurant. They cook quickly and, for me, are one of those things that taste far better than they look. You will need some bread for mopping up the sauce and a green salad or a dish of sautéed spinach or other wilted greens such as turnip tops in olive oil. The livers have to be excellent: young, fresh and plump. Clean them very well before you start cooking and get rid of anything that might taste bitter.

Make the tomato piri piri sauce on page 15 if you don't have some ready for use. Heat the butter in a non-stick frying pan until it turns golden and starts to smell delicious. Throw in the oregano and let it sauté for a moment, then when it smells good add the livers. Fry until deep golden brown and a bit crusty, then turn them gently. Season with salt and pepper and pour in the lemon juice.

Add the tomato piri piri sauce, put the lid on the pan and let it bubble up to mingle all the flavours and cook the livers through. Add a few drops of water if it seems too dry as it bubbles.

Taste and add ground piri piri if you want it hotter. If you won't be serving this immediately, leave the pan with the lid on and just heat through with a few drops of water.
Serves 4

PASTEIS DE BACALHAU
— codfish cakes —

375 G (13 OZ) BACALHAU (*SALT COD*), *soaked* • 500 G (1 LB 2 OZ) POTATOES, *scrubbed but unpeeled* •
OLIVE OIL, *for frying* • 1 SHALLOT OR ½ SMALL ONION, FINELY CHOPPED •
1 GARLIC CLOVE, *finely chopped* • A *small twist of* PAPRIKA • A *grating of* NUTMEG •
1 TABLESPOON *chopped* CORIANDER (*CILANTRO*) • 1 TABLESPOON *chopped* PARSLEY •
1 *LARGE* EGG, *lightly beaten*

These have a wonderful delicate flavour (if you prefer more 'coddiness', add a little extra bacalhau) and can be made, in more traditional fashion, without the coriander. You can easily make a meal of these: a pile of bright green broad (fava) beans, blanched and dressed in olive oil; black olives and boiled egg wedges; and a batch of these with lemon wedges.

Before you use the salt cod you need to soak it to remove the excess salt. Rinse the cod pieces first, then put them in a large bowl with enough water to completely immerse them. Cover the bowl and refrigerate, changing the water 3–4 times a day. Ask your fishmonger how long you need to soak the cod (it's usually about 2–3 days). If you're unsure, test the cod by breaking off a small fleck, rinsing and tasting it. The tail part is always a bit more salty. In some places you can buy ready-soaked salt cod which is very reliable and convenient.

Drain the bacalhau and shred into a bowl, discarding the skin and bones. Bring a pan of water to the boil, add the shredded fish and boil for 2 minutes or so (taste a little flake of fish to check it's not still too salty: if it is, change the water and boil for a few more minutes). Drain very well.

Meanwhile, boil the potatoes in lightly salted water for about 15 minutes, or until just soft — don't overcook them or the fish cakes will be too soft. Drain, cool a bit, peel and mash the potatoes. Add the shredded cod and mash that in, too.

Heat 1 tablespoon olive oil in a small pan and sauté the shallot until golden. Add the garlic and cook until you start to smell it. Scrape into the mash. Add salt and pepper, the paprika, nutmeg, coriander, parsley and beaten egg and mix until smooth and firm. Taste for seasoning.

Use two tablespoons to make quenelles of the mixture, passing it from spoon to spoon several times until you have a very firm, compact oval cake. Shape them all and chill them for a while to firm them before you start frying, so they don't collapse in the pan.

Pour enough oil into a large non-stick frying pan to come halfway up the fish cakes when they are frying. When the oil is hot, gently add a batch of cakes, turning them only when they have a good golden crust underneath. They will crumble if you turn them too soon. If they are over-browning you may need to reduce the heat a touch.

Lift them out onto a plate lined with kitchen paper to absorb the excess oil, then onto a clean platter. Salt and serve with lemon if you like. Best warm, but lovely at room temperature, too. *Makes about 20*

I went for a walk with Mini and we discovered the ginjeria. It is an especially beautiful old shop, with another further on down the street. We drank our ginjinha from small, round-bottomed shot glasses — there were two or three ginjas floating in my glass. Mini had a capilé, which also came in a shot glass but is a syrup made from many juices and rinds and diluted with fizzy water. Our friend Rachele says that in autumn they drink one that is made from chestnuts.

AMEIJOAS A BULHAO PATO

— clams with coriander, garlic and lemon —

1 KG (2 LB 4 OZ) CLAMS *IN SHELLS* · 2 *THIN* LEMON SLICES, *quartered* · 2 GARLIC CLOVES, *chopped* ·
2 TABLESPOONS OLIVE OIL · 1 TABLESPOON BUTTER · A *pinch or two of ground* PIRI PIRI ·
JUICE OF 1 LEMON · 2 TABLESPOONS *chopped* CORIANDER (*CILANTRO*)

Clams like these are everywhere in Portugal. Don't buy them too small — unless you're going to serve them with rice or pasta you'll find them too fiddly to eat. You could add some cubes of chouriço and green pepper to the onion sauté, and instead of lemon juice you could use a good splash of whatever white wine you're drinking. Your clams will probably have been purged of sand already but check with the fishmonger, otherwise you'll need to soak them for a day in a colander standing in well-salted water, changing the water several times.

If you've been soaking your clams, give them a good swirl in the water, rinse them, drain and leave in the colander. Put the lemon slices and garlic in a large pot with the oil and butter. Sauté until the buttery oil is golden, the lemon is softened and you start to smell the garlic. Add the piri piri and cook for a few seconds more, taking care not to burn the garlic.

Add the clams and lemon juice and season well. Turn the heat up high, put the lid on and cook for 10 minutes or so until the clam shells open. If necessary, put the lid back on for a couple of minutes and give them another chance, then discard any that are still stubbornly closed. Shuffle the clams around by rocking the pot, add the coriander and shuffle again. Turn off the heat and leave with the lid on for a bit, then serve with good bread and a bowl for the shells. *Serves 4*

AZORES OCTOPUS

3 *SMALL OR* 1 *LARGE* OCTOPUS (ABOUT 500 G/1 LB 2 OZ) · 3 TABLESPOONS OLIVE OIL ·
1 *SMALL* ONION, *chopped* · 1 CELERY STALK, *chopped* · 2 GARLIC CLOVES, *chopped* ·
3 TABLESPOONS *chopped* PARSLEY · 1 *large* OREGANO OR THYME *SPRIG* · *A pinch of ground* PIRI PIRI ·
2 CLOVES · 3 TABLESPOONS WHITE WINE · 2 TABLESPOONS AGUARDENTE *OR BRANDY*

This is lovely as a petisco before a seafood main course, or even before something like grilled chicken. Serve it with bread — toasted or not — and in individual portions or on a big platter with some skewers or toothpicks. You could even add rice and water to the octopus pan towards the end of the cooking time to make a lovely octopus rice. You can make this beforehand and serve at room temperature, or keep in the pot and add a few drops of water to heat through before serving.

To clean the octopus, cut between the head and tentacles, just below the eyes. Grasp the body and push the beak up and out through the centre of the tentacles with your finger. Cut the eyes from the head. To clean the head, carefully slit through one side, avoiding the ink sac, and scrape out any gut. Rinse under running water to remove any grit. Cut the head into chunks and the tentacles into rounds of about 2 cm (3/4 inch), leaving the thinner ends a bit longer or they will curl up and become nothing.

Heat the olive oil in a heavy-based pot. Sauté the onion and, when it starts to colour, add the celery and continue to sauté until both are soft and nicely golden.

Add the garlic, parsley and herb sprig and cook until you start to smell the garlic, then add the octopus.

Cook for quite a while (10 minutes or more) until most of the liquid has evaporated and it looks syrupy in the pot. Add the piri piri and cloves and season with salt and pepper.

Add the wine, aguardente and 125 ml (4 fl oz/½ cup) of water and bring to the boil. Lower the heat, then cover and simmer for 45 minutes until most of the liquid has evaporated and the octopus has a lovely colour and looks almost caramelised (but take care it doesn't burn and catch on the pot).

Taste and adjust the seasoning. If the octopus is too firm, add more water and continue cooking, covered, until it is tender and there is very little liquid in the pot.

Serves 3–4

CALAMARI WITH LEMON, GARLIC AND PIRI PIRI

400 G (14 OZ) BABY CALAMARI · 30 G (1 OZ) BUTTER · 1 *scant* TEASPOON DRIED OREGANO ·
2 GARLIC CLOVES, *finely chopped* · *juice of* 1 LEMON · *a pinch of ground* PIRI PIRI ·
1 TABLESPOON *chopped* PARSLEY

This is a very tasty petisco to have with bread and a couple of other plates for sharing. Or you could make a larger quantity and serve with a warm salad, some blanched spinach or other greens and maybe boiled new potatoes or tomato rice — you won't even need to increase the amount of dressing. You will need a good non-stick pan here and the hottest, highest heat for cooking or the calamari will produce a lot of steam and become tough. Use soft, tender, baby calamari. I had about ten and they were each just 6 cm (2½ inches) long.

To prepare the calamari, firmly pull the head and innards from the body and wash the body well. Cut off the head just below the eyes, leaving the tentacles in one piece if they're small. Discard the head, pull the transparent quill out of the body and rinse out the tube.

Peel off the outer membrane and slice the tube into three or four rings.

Put the butter into a hot pan and heat until it sizzles. Add the oregano and cook for a moment until it smells good. Add the tubes and tentacles and cook on the highest heat until all the liquid evaporates. Sprinkle with salt and a little pepper and, when it's all turning golden, turn with a wooden spoon and scrape up any bits stuck to the pan.

Add the garlic and turn through until you start to smell it. Add the lemon juice and however much piri piri you like. Let it bubble up, check the seasoning and stir in the parsley over the heat for just a moment longer. Add a touch more butter and lemon to the pan if you like more sauce. Serve hot in the pan with bread. *Serves 2–3*

Starters
AND SOUPS

arroz

SEAFOOD RICE

150 G (5½ OZ) *SMALL* CLAMS *in shells* · 8 RAW PRAWNS · 8 MUSSELS · 4 SMALL SQUID ·
4 *small* MOSCARDINI *or baby* OCTOPUS · 4 CRAB LEGS · 125 ML (4 FL OZ/½ CUP) OLIVE OIL ·
1 SMALL ONION, *chopped* · ½ GREEN PEPPER (*CAPSICUM*), *chopped* · 4 GARLIC CLOVES, *chopped* ·
A HANDFUL OF *chopped* PARSLEY · 250 ML (9 FL OZ/1 CUP) TOMATO PASSATA ·
¼ TEASPOON GROUND PIRI PIRI · 250 G (9 OZ) *PARBOILED VARIETY OF* LONG-GRAIN RICE ·
125 ML (4 FL OZ/½ CUP) WHITE WINE, *plus 3 tablespoons extra* ·
750 ML (26 FL OZ/3 CUPS) *HOT* VEGETABLE STOCK · 1 BAY LEAF · 1 TABLESPOON BUTTER

You can easily halve this to serve two. It might seem fiddly because the different seafood need different treatments, but once you have cleaned everything it is really no fuss and bother. In Setúbal this was served in a tiny pot which I loved. At the end of the meal I asked if I could buy one and, this being Portugal, the restaurant owner not only said yes, but, 'offerta, no buy!' (It's the pot in the photograph.)

Your clams will probably have been purged of sand already but check with your fishmonger, otherwise you'll need to soak them for a day in a colander standing in a bowl of well-salted water, changing the water several times. If you're at all worried that they might still be harbouring some sand, steam them in a separate pan and add them at the end.

You can use a good stock cube or make a simple vegetable stock by simmering a peeled onion, carrot, celery stalk and seasoning in about 4 cupfuls of water for a while.

If you've been soaking your clams, give them a good swirl in the water, rinse them, drain and leave in the colander. Remove the heads from the prawns but leave the shells on the bodies. Make a shallow cut down the back of each one and devein them. Snip off the legs.

'De-beard' the mussels by pulling away those fiddly bits of algae that stick out. Cut them off with scissors or a knife if you can't detach them, then scrub the shells well with a wire brush to dislodge evidence of the sea. At this stage you need to discard any mussels that are open and don't close when you give them a tap.

To prepare the squid, firmly pull the head and innards from the body and wash the body well. Cut off the head just below the eyes, leaving the tentacles in one piece if they're small. Discard the head, pull the transparent quill out of the body and rinse out the tube. Peel off the outer membrane and slice the tube into thin rings.

To clean the moscardini, cut between the head and tentacles. Grasp the body and push the beak up and out through the centre of the tentacles with your finger. Leave the tentacles whole if they're small, or cut in half if large. The heads can be left whole or halved if large. Crack the crab legs so they take in the flavours.

Heat 4 tablespoons of the oil in a large pot and sauté the onion and green pepper. Add half the garlic and half the parsley and, when you can smell the garlic, add the moscardini. Turn through, let it bubble and then add the tomato and piri piri. Simmer for 5 minutes, then add the rice and stir it around in the pot for a minute, letting it pick up all the flavours. Add the white wine and let it fizzle and evaporate. When it has bubbled away, add the crab legs and 2 cups of the hot stock. Let the rice simmer for 10–15 minutes, adding the rest of the stock towards the end of this time — the rice won't be completely soft but will finish cooking later.

Meanwhile, heat the remaining 2 tablespoons of olive oil in a frying pan. Add the remaining garlic and cook until you can smell it. Add the rest of the parsley and the bay leaf, then add the squid rings. Simmer for a few minutes, then add the prawns and simmer for a couple of minutes. Add the clams and mussels and the extra white wine. Season with salt and pepper and cover. Cook over high heat for a few minutes until the clams and mussels open. Turn off the heat and leave covered for now.

When the rice is ready, turn the seafood with its liquid through the rice and stir in the butter. Taste for seasoning and leave covered for the rice to finish cooking. Discard any unopened clams or mussels. Serve with plenty of napkins and finger bowls.

Serves 4 (or 2 as a main course)

OCTOPUS FEIJOADA

500-600 G (ABOUT 1 LB 4 OZ) OCTOPUS · 400 G (14 OZ) *DRIED* BORLOTTI BEANS *or*
KIDNEY BEANS, *soaked overnight* · 2 BAY LEAVES ·
50 G (1³/₄ OZ) CHOURIÇO SAUSAGE, *casing removed if thick, quartered then sliced* ·
4 TABLESPOONS OLIVE OIL · 1 LARGE ONION, *chopped* · 1 CELERY STALK ·
2 *SMALL* CARROTS, *peeled and chopped* · 3 GARLIC CLOVES, *chopped* · 2 *tablespoons chopped* PARSLEY ·
A *pinch of ground* PIRI PIRI · 125 ML (4 FL OZ/¹/₂ CUP) RED WINE · 2 *tablespoons* PUREED TOMATO

I found this at the sardine festival in the Algarve and was thrilled by it. I asked the lady who was cooking if she could write down what was in it. From my notes it looks like: *frita-se a cebola picada. Tomate maduro, depois do refugado junta — se opolvo ja cozido e o feijoa, depois junta-se o camarão (o feijoa ja cozido)*. So, she had prawns in hers (and you can add those if you like) but I used just octopus.

To clean the octopus, cut between the head and tentacles, just below the eyes. Grasp the body and push the beak up and out through the centre of the tentacles with your finger. Cut the eyes from the head. To clean the head, carefully slit through one side, avoiding the ink sac, and scrape out any gut. Rinse under running water to remove any grit. Cut the head into chunks and the tentacles into lengths of 3–4 cm (1¹/₂ inches) on the diagonal.

Drain the beans into a large pan, cover with a lot of fresh water and bring to the boil. Lower the heat and skim off any froth. Add a bay leaf and the chouriço and simmer for about 50 minutes until tender, seasoning well in the last 10 minutes of cooking.

Meanwhile, heat the olive oil in a large pan. Sauté the onion, celery and carrot until soft and golden. Add the octopus and the other bay leaf and cook until all the liquid has evaporated. Season with salt and pepper, add the garlic, parsley and piri piri and, when you can smell the garlic and there is very little sticky sauce, add the wine.

Let it bubble up, then add the tomato, smashing it to dissolve in the sauce. Add a cupful of water and bring to the boil. Cover the pan, lower the heat and simmer for about an hour until the octopus is lovely and tender and there is a good amount of thickened sauce with it. If it looks too dry at any time, add more water and continue simmering.

The octopus and beans should be ready at more or less the same time. Drain the beans, saving the cooking water. Stir the beans into the octopus and its sauce and add about a cupful of the bean cooking water. Let it simmer together for 5 minutes or so for the flavours to mingle. Check the seasoning and serve warm, scattered with chopped parsley.

Serves 4–6 (or 2–3 as a main course)

Yesterday I went to Porto. What a magic conglomeration of tiles and higgledy-piggledy streets lined with crumbling azulejos, and not a straight line in sight. I felt I needed a glass of port to set me right. I had the feeling, as I stared across the river at the factories and the man in his cloak, that I shouldn't leave Porto. It was as if time had stood still for me and was taking a long breath before giving an encore. That bridge, the people softly milling about, the new bridge being built... the gentleness of it all.

marisco

SEAFOOD IN CATAPLANA

10 *SMALL CLAMS in shells* · 6 BLACK MUSSELS · 240 G (9 OZ) *small* MOSCARDINI OR *baby* OCTOPUS ·
6 RAW PRAWNS · 2 *small firm* FISH FILLETS (*SUCH AS SNAPPER, MACKEREL, HALIBUT OR MONKFISH*) ·
4 TABLESPOONS OLIVE OIL · 1 SMALL ONION, *chopped* ·
½ RED OR GREEN PEPPER (*CAPSICUM*), *roughly chopped* · 3 GARLIC CLOVES, *chopped* ·
200 G (7 OZ) *tinned chopped* TOMATOES · ½ TEASPOON GROUND PIRI PIRI ·
125 ML (4 FL OZ/½ CUP) WHITE WINE · JUICE *OF 1 SMALL* LEMON ·
2 TABLESPOONS *chopped* CORIANDER (*CILANTRO*)

A cataplana is a traditional Portuguese domed copper pot with a tight-fitting lid that has a clasp on the side to lock it as you cook. This means it can be flipped upside down halfway through for even cooking. Assuming you don't have your own cataplana, use a wok or a wide non-stick pot with a lid (and don't turn it upside down!). This is a very elastic recipe that is easily adjusted to suit your own tastes — all clams or no clams, more lemon, less coriander, more chilli and so on. You can also add half a cup or so of port and serve with Portuguese floury rolls, if possible, or white rice. Your clams will probably have been purged of sand already but check with your fishmonger,

otherwise you'll need to soak them for a day in a colander standing in a bowl of well-salted water, changing the water several times.

Set your table with crusty bread and a good salad and make sure the wine is chilling in the fridge. You will also need an empty bowl or two for the shells.

Prepare all your seafood. If you've been soaking your clams, give them a good swirl in the water, rinse them, drain and leave in the colander. Before you start cooking the mussels you need to 'de-beard' them by pulling away those fiddly bits of algae that stick out. Cut them off with scissors or a knife if you can't detach them, then scrub the shells well with a wire brush to dislodge evidence of the sea. At this stage you need to discard any mussels that are open and don't close when you give them a tap.

To clean the moscardini, cut between the head and tentacles. Grasp the body and push the beak up and out through the centre of the tentacles with your finger. Leave the tentacles whole if they're small, or cut in half if large. The heads can be left whole or halved if large.

Make a slit down the back of each prawn and remove the dark vein.

Rinse and drain all the seafood well and pat the fish pieces dry with kitchen paper.

Heat the oil in a large pot and sauté the onion until golden and sticky. Add the pepper and carry on cooking. Add the garlic and, when you start to smell it, add the tomatoes and moscardini, crushing the tomatoes with your wooden spoon. Season with 1 teaspoon of salt

and simmer for about 10 minutes until the liquid is reducing and the moscardini have cooked a bit.

Stir in the piri piri, cook for a moment and then add the rest of the seafood, the wine and lemon juice and a couple of twists of pepper. Put the lid on tightly, the heat on high, and let it all come up to a strong boil. After 5 minutes or so, mix through quickly, lower the heat a dash (the clams and mussels should already be opening) and cook for another 5 minutes until the prawns are bright pink, the clams and mussels open (discard any that haven't opened by now), the moscardini white and tender and the fish just cooked through. There should be a good amount of sauce mingling at the bottom of the pot.

Stir in the coriander, check again for seasoning, put the lid back on and take it to the table. *Serves 4 (or 2 as a main course)*

SALT COD, CORIANDER, GARLIC AND BREAD SOUP

200 G (7 OZ) BACALHAU (*SALT COD*), *soaked* · 1 SHALLOT, *peeled* · A FEW PEPPERCORNS ·
1 BAY LEAF · 4 GARLIC CLOVES, *roughly chopped* · A PINCH OF PAPRIKA ·
2–3 TABLESPOONS *chopped* CORIANDER (*CILANTRO*) · 2 TABLESPOONS OLIVE OIL *plus extra to drizzle* ·
2 EGG YOLKS *AT ROOM TEMPERATURE* · A LITTLE NUTMEG ·
2 SLICES COUNTRY-STYLE BREAD, *halved*

This, if you love coriander, is a beautiful thing to serve as a starter before a fish main course (even a main of bacalhau!). The toasted bread softens with all the garlic and coriander and bacalhau flavours in your bowl. You can tear in some more bread and let it soak up the broth to make an *açorda* — a bread stew rather than a soup, if you like. Before you use the salt cod you need to soak it to remove the excess salt. Rinse the cod first, then put it in a large bowl with enough water to completely immerse. Cover and refrigerate, changing the water 3–4 times a day. Ask your fishmonger how long you need to soak the cod (it's usually about 2–3 days). If you're unsure, test the cod by breaking off a small fleck, rinsing and tasting it. The tail part is always a bit more salty. In some places you can buy convenient ready-soaked salt cod.

Drain the bacalhau and put in a pot with the shallot, 3 or 4 peppercorns and the bay leaf. Cover with water, bring to the boil and simmer for about 10 minutes until the fish is cooked.

Lift the fish onto a plate, remove the skin and bones and flake into large pieces. Strain the cooking broth and return about 500 ml (17 fl oz/2 cups) of the broth to the clean pot.

Crush the garlic, paprika, a twist of pepper, half the coriander and 1 tablespoon of the oil to a paste with a mortar and pestle or a spice grinder.

Heat the other tablespoon of olive oil in a small pan. Add the paste and stir through the bacalhau to coat well in the paste.

Meanwhile, heat up the strained broth and whisk the yolks in a metal bowl. Add a ladleful of hot broth to the egg yolks and whisk until smooth, then tip back into the pan of broth over low heat. Cook for just a few moments and taste for seasoning (you may not need extra salt). Add a sprinkling of nutmeg.

Toast the bread until crisp and put into soup bowls. Ladle soup over the bread, make a pile of cod on top and sprinkle with pepper and coriander. Serve with a drizzle of olive oil and a sprinkling of paprika, if you like. *Serves 2*

cold soup

GASPACHO A PORTUGUESA

1 *SMALL RED* ONION, *finely chopped* · COARSE SALT · ABOUT 400 G (14 OZ) *very ripe* TOMATOES ·
1 CUCUMBER, *peeled* · 1 GREEN PEPPER (*CAPSICUM*), *seeded and chopped* ·
1 RED PEPPER (*CAPSICUM*), *seeded and chopped* · 1 CELERY STALK *WITH LEAVES, chopped* ·
2 *SMALL FRESH* BAY LEAVES · 1–2 TABLESPOONS *chopped* PARSLEY · ³/₄ TEASPOON *DRIED* OREGANO ·
1 GARLIC CLOVE, *peeled and a bit squashed* · 3 TABLESPOONS OLIVE OIL ·
2–3 TABLESPOONS RED WINE VINEGAR, *or more to taste* · ABOUT 1 TABLESPOON PORT ·
PIRI PIRI SAUCE OR OIL, *to serve*

Piri piri for serving is a must here. The gaspacho I had was nice and cold and had all different sizes of vegetables — but none too big — a little oil, some oregano and a splash of vinegar. I had hoped for a port vinegar for this, so mingling the red wine vinegar with a little port lifted the gaspacho to new heights. Add more vinegar if you like; keep tasting to get the balance right for your own tastes. Serve with crusty bread, or just put some torn bread in the bowl.

⤳

Put the onion in a small bowl, cover with cold water, scatter with a teaspoon of coarse salt and leave for an hour or so. Prepare the tomatoes by peeling off the skin with a small sharp knife. Cut them in half through the middle and hold over a fine sieve, which in turn is over a bowl to catch the juice. Remove the seeds (dropping them into the sieve), then dice the tomatoes.

Hold the cucumber upright and divide into 4 thick slices vertically. Then cut each fat slice into long batons and chop these. The very middle seedy part can be removed if you like, or left if you prefer.

Put into a big bowl (even the one that you will use for serving) and add 2 teaspoons or so of coarse salt. Mix in the chopped peppers and celery, the bay leaves and chopped tomatoes

with their juice. Add 500 ml (17 fl oz/2 cups) of cold water and stir in the parsley and oregano. Grind some pepper over the top, cover and leave in the fridge for an hour or so.

Put the garlic clove in a small bowl with the oil, vinegar and port and leave to marinate. Take the gaspacho out of the fridge, add the oil and vinegar (discarding the garlic) and the rinsed and drained onion. Mix well, then taste for the seasonings and adjust any flavours that need it. Keep in the fridge if you won't be serving immediately. Definitely serve with several splashes of a piri piri sauce or oil.

Makes about 1.5 litres (52 fl oz/6 cups)

I chose a cervejaria at random in rua de Rosa and settled myself and my shopping onto the bar stool, between a builder and a man who was shouting at the world, and ordered a cold glass of white wine. Up came the wine and with it came a tiny plate of lupini beans and another tiny plate next to it for the skins. I picked my way through some as I watched around me and then asked the barman a question which obviously got me into his good books, because he scooped up a handful of olives and piled them onto my already miniature lupini plate with a lovely moustachioed smile, and didnt even blink when a couple of olives rolled off towards the builder and the shouter. I asked for a menu and liked it so much that I ordered a meal and moved to a table. I had the prawn açorda and it was delicious — rich and beautiful.

GREEN BEAN AND POTATO SOUP

2 *SMALL* LEEKS · ABOUT 400 G (14 OZ) LAMB OR BEEF KNUCKLE BONES ·
4 TABLESPOONS OLIVE OIL · 1 ONION, *chopped* · 2 GARLIC CLOVES, *chopped* ·
1 KG (2 LB 4 OZ) GREEN BEANS, *topped and cut into short lengths* ·
600 G (1 LB 5 OZ) POTATOES, *peeled and cut into big chunks*

This I made with my friend, Corinne, a marvellous cook who knows a lot about Portuguese cooking. The two main ingredients are abundant in Portugal — the country has beans, beans and more beans, and they are always lovely. And in my guide book it said: 'If you want your potatoes to grow, you have to talk to them in Portuguese'. This makes a rather army-style amount of thick soup that will probably give you two days' worth — you could send some over to your neighbours if you find you have too much, or just halve the quantities.

Halve the leeks and slice them up thinly. Put them in a bowl of water, slosh them around with your hands to make sure there is no grit inside, and then drain them in a colander.

Rinse the lamb or beef to get rid of any stray bits of bone and pat dry. Heat the olive oil in a large wide pot and brown the bones well, cooking on both sides until deep golden. Add the onion and leeks around the bones and sauté until those too are nicely golden and well cooked. Add the garlic and cook until you start to smell it, then add the beans, turning them through and seasoning with about 3 teaspoons of coarse salt and some pepper.

Add about 1.5 litres (52 fl oz/6 cups) of hot water, partly cover the pan and simmer for an hour or so, stirring a couple of times. Add the potato and another 500 ml (17 fl oz/2 cups) or so of hot water, depending on how much it looks like it needs. Simmer, covered, for another 30 minutes until the potatoes are nicely soft but not collapsing.

Remove the bones and ladle out about a litre (35 fl oz/4 cups) of soup — mainly beans and liquid, but a few potatoes to make it nice and thick. Purée this, then return to the pot so the soup is a mixture of chunky and smooth.

Taste for seasoning and serve hot. If anyone wants to, they can pick the bones or you can just use them just for flavouring.

Makes nearly 3 litres (104 fl oz /12 cups)

ACORDA OF PRAWNS

8 RAW PRAWNS · 3 TABLESPOONS OLIVE OIL · 1 SHALLOT, *peeled and halved* ·
2 GARLIC CLOVES, *1 chopped, the other peeled but left whole* · 1 BAY LEAF ·
A FEW PARSLEY *STEMS AND LEAVES* · 1 SMALL CARROT, *peeled and halved* ·
1 *SMALL* CELERY STALK · COARSE SALT · *a few* PEPPERCORNS · *A pinch of ground sweet* PAPRIKA ·
1-2 TABLESPOONS *chopped* PARSLEY · 3 TABLESPOONS WHITE WINE ·
ABOUT 120 G (4 OZ) *yesterday's white country-style* BREAD, *crusts removed, broken into small pieces* ·
1 EGG YOLK, *optional*

An *açorda* is a soupy casserole thickened with mashed bread. It can be flavoured simply with garlic and tomato but is often made with seafood. You can whisk an egg yolk into this at the very last moment before serving, which is how I ate it in Lisbon. It makes the dish much richer and creamier, so it's up to you whether to add it. Use white country-style bread, such as Portuguese rolls or ciabatta — yesterday's loaf so that it's just on the verge of staleness. You can change the direction of this dramatically by adding freshly chopped coriander or any other herbs (I love thyme, too, here).

Peel and devein the prawns, keeping all the heads and shells. Make a broth first: heat a tablespoon of the olive oil in a small pan and sauté half the shallot, the whole garlic clove, bay leaf, parsley, carrot, celery and the prawn heads and shells until it starts to smell good. Add 500 ml (17 fl oz/2 cups) of hot water, some salt and a few peppercorns. Bring to the boil, cover and simmer for 20 minutes. Strain.

Chop the other shallot half. Heat the rest of the oil in a small heavy-based pan and sauté the shallot until golden. Add the peeled prawns, season with salt, pepper and a little paprika and sauté over high heat until turning golden and crusty. Add the garlic and parsley and continue cooking until you can smell the garlic. Lift the prawns out onto a plate.

Pour the wine into the pan and let it bubble up to reduce. Add the pieces of bread, turning them through so they sauté a bit and collect the pan flavours. Add some of your broth (you will have about 1³/₄ cups but you may not need to add it all) and simmer, bashing and mixing with a wooden spoon so the bread breaks up completely and you get a thick stew.

Taste for seasoning and stir in the prawns just before serving. Take off the heat and quickly stir in the beaten egg yolk if you are using it. Serve hot, maybe with a drizzle of piri piri oil. *Serves 2*

FENNEL SOUP

2 FENNEL BULBS (ABOUT 500 G/1 LB 2 OZ) · ABOUT 550 G (1 LB 4 OZ) *SHORT* PORK RIBS ·
4 TABLESPOONS OLIVE OIL · 125 ML (4 FL OZ/½ CUP) WHITE WINE · 1 ONION, *chopped* ·
3 GARLIC CLOVES, *chopped* · 2 BAY LEAVES · 450 G (1 LB) POTATOES, *peeled and sliced* ·
CRUSHED DRIED WILD FENNEL FLOWERS, *if you have some*

In the Azores they tend to use just the feathery fronds of the fennel — I used the whole vegetable and loved it too. If you can get some, dried wild fennel flowers crushed between your fingers at the end will add a shower of magic. If you can't find the flowers, choose a couple of bulbs that have some lovely feathery fronds for chopping into the soup before serving.

Preheat your oven to 210°C (415°F/Gas 6–7). Trim the fennel bulbs, keeping a handful of the feathery fronds. Halve the fennel from the top down, and then divide each half into 3 or 4 thick pieces that are a comfortable size for roasting. Cut the pork ribs into individual ribs and trim off any excess fat (you should get about 12 ribs).

Put the ribs in a roasting tin and splash with half the olive oil. Roast for 20 minutes and then add the fennel, turning through the oil. Put back in the oven for 25 minutes, or until the ribs are roasted and the fennel looks golden here and there. Season with salt and pepper, add the wine and roast for another

5–10 minutes until it is bubbling up and has evaporated a bit. Take out 8 of the ribs and set aside for serving later.

Meanwhile, heat the remaining oil in a large soup pot and sauté the onion (it may not seem much oil but the soup will get the rest of the oil from the ribs), stirring often. Add the garlic and bay leaves and stir until you start to smell the garlic.

Tip in the remaining 4 ribs, the fennel and all the roasting juices from the tin, the potato slices and some salt and pepper. Add 1.5 litres (52 fl oz/6 cups) of hot water, cover and bring to the boil, then lower the heat and simmer, covered, for about 20 minutes until the potatoes are cooked through.

Lift out the ribs (you won't serve these ones) and remove the bay leaves. Purée the rest of the soup and taste for seasoning. Add some of the chopped fennel fronds and flowers, simmer for a couple of minutes and then serve hot with a roasted rib or two on the side and a scattering of pepper.

Makes 2 litres (70 fl oz/8 cups)

sopa

CARROT SOUP

2 LEEKS · 4 TABLESPOONS OLIVE OIL · 2 GARLIC CLOVES, *chopped* ·
800 G (1 LB 12 OZ) CARROTS, *peeled and cut into chunks* ·
1.25 LITRES (44 FL OZ/5 CUPS) *HOT* VEGETABLE STOCK · 500 G (1 LB 2 OZ) POTATOES, *peeled*

I have seen rice added to this, but I actually love this simple recipe that is creamy, soft and sweet from the carrots. The soup will look as bright and healthy as the carrots you start off with. If you like, you can add a beef bone at the start for flavour. You can use a good stock cube or make a vegetable stock by simmering a peeled onion, carrot, celery stalk and seasoning in about 4 cupfuls of water for a while.

Halve the leeks and slice them up thinly. Put them in a bowl of water, slosh them around with your hands to make sure there is no grit inside, and then drain them in a colander. Heat the olive oil in a large wide pot and sauté the leeks until they are soft and starting to turn golden, but take care that they don't darken too much.

Add the garlic and cook until you start to smell it. Add the carrots and turn through the oil. Add the hot stock and some salt and pepper and bring to the boil.

Cut the potatoes into big chunks and add to the pot. Bring back to the boil, then reduce to a simmer, cover the pot and cook for about 40 minutes.

Turn off the heat. Ladle out 2 heaped slotted spoonfuls of mainly potatoes and some carrots (trying to leave everything else behind as best as you can!) and set aside. Purée the soup in the pot until smooth, adding a dash of extra stock or water if it seems too thick, then stir the unpuréed potato and carrot back into the soup. Taste for seasoning before serving, or leave for a while and reheat gently. *Serves 4*

- The coast by fast car -

Our intention was to travel to Cascais by train. But the taxi driver talked us into letting him take us all the way there for not much of a fee. We agreed, but then he drove like a madman, leaving me wishing we'd taken the train after all, my eyes glued to his speedometer wishing time away. 'No problem,' he kept saying. (Of course it was no problem to him — these were not his children.) We arrived clean and lean and jumped out straight into a local restaurant where the older-looking owner was shuffling up and down, tending to his customers with a smile. We sat at the back near an elderly Portuguese lady lunching alone — always a very encouraging sign. The food was delicious. A small metal army-looking bowl of soup for the kids, with chunks of cabbage and carrot and a good taste of meat and chouriço although there was none evident. They had a different soup every day, the man told us. We ordered grilled squid and grilled sardines — both with boiled potatoes. Mine had lots of gold olive oil over it and big flecks of very bright chopped parsley. On the way to our table I had noticed an older lady in the kitchen (probably the owner's wife) and a lady who looked like she could have been from Brazil. This all made me comfortable. The bread (a forewarning as to how any restaurant will be) was so good that we asked if we could take the rest of our basket away. So they brought one of their plastic bags that seem to have special colours for some reason in Portugal.

Teresa

VEGETABLE SOUP

2 TABLESPOONS OLIVE OIL · 2 WHITE ONIONS, *chopped* ·
2 LARGE CARROTS, *peeled, 1 chopped and the other halved* ·
225 G (8 OZ) ZUCCHINI (*COURGETTES*) or baby marrow, chopped ·
700 G (1 LB 9 OZ) POTATOES, *peeled and thickly sliced* ·
3 HANDFULS OF SPINACH, *CHARD (SILVERBEET) OR KALE LEAVES, left whole or torn if they are large*

I went to the fruit and vegetable market in the Algarve and asked them to give me whatever vegetables a Portuguese lady would use to make a soup, please. They gave me these exact amounts for one family. When I got back to the house Teresa arrived to cook with me. And she knew exactly what to do with them. Both Teresa and the greengrocer lady said they might have put in a beef bone, too, maybe just a knuckle or two for flavour and then lifted it out. This is simple, lovely and healthy — the kind of soup I want to eat once a week forever.

Heat the oil in a large pot and sauté the onion, chopped carrot and zucchini until softened. Add 1.25 litres (44 fl oz/5 cups) of cold water (enough to cover the spinach to be put in later). Season well, add the potatoes and halved carrot, stir and bring to the boil. Cover and reduce the heat a dash. Cook for 15 minutes, then check there is still enough water. Stir in the spinach, cover again, bring back to the boil and cook for 10 minutes more. The potatoes should be soft but not collapsing.

Lift out most of the potatoes and pieces of carrot with a slotted spoon, mash well and return to the pot. Stir and leave covered until ready to serve (it's best not quite piping hot). Add water if it needs thinning, but it should be more like a thin stew than a thick soup. Serve with bread.

Makes about 2 litres (70 fl oz/8 cups)

TOMATO SOUP WITH CORIANDER AND POACHED EGG

3 TABLESPOONS OLIVE OIL, *plus some extra* • 1 RED ONION, *chopped* •
3 GARLIC CLOVES, *1 peeled and slightly squashed, 2 chopped* • 1 BAY LEAF •
650 G (1 LB 7 OZ) *VERY RIPE* TOMATOES, *peeled and thickly sliced* •
4 *THICKISH SLICES* CHOURICO SAUSAGE OR LINGUICA • 4 *THINNISH SLICES* PRESUNTO OR PROSCIUTTO •
1 *THICK* SLICE OF BREAD • 4 EGGS, *at room temperature* •
1 TABLESPOON *chopped* CORIANDER (*CILANTRO*), *plus a few extra leaves*

This is a bowl of beauty and lovely in summer when tomatoes are at their best. For me, the coriander makes this but it is sometimes served without. If you were making this in true Portuguese style you'd break the eggs straight into the soup pan and poach them in there, but, if you find the thought a bit intimidating, poach them in a separate pan of water. Peel the tomatoes by scoring a cross in the base of each one, dipping them for a few seconds into a bowl of boiling water, then putting them into cold water. You will be able to peel the skin away from the cross. If you like, cut them in half and squeeze out the seeds.

Heat the oil in a stockpot and sauté the onion until golden and sticky. Add the chopped garlic and bay leaf and cook until you start to smell the garlic, then add the tomatoes. Sauté until the water from the tomatoes reduces and they start cooking in the oil and taking the flavours from the pan. Season very generously.

Add 750 ml (26 fl oz/3 cups) hot water and bring back to the boil. Cover the pan, lower the heat and simmer for 10 minutes. Turn off the heat, remove the bay and ladle out 3 slotted spoonfuls of tomato. Purée the rest of the soup until smooth. Taste for seasoning and return the tomato chunks to the pan.

Heat enough oil to cover the bottom of a small frying pan. Fry the chouriço and presunto slices, in batches if needed, until very crisp and golden. Lift out, keeping the oil. Cut the bread into rough cubes and fry in the same oil with the garlic clove until lightly golden.

To poach the eggs, add a dash of vinegar to a pot of lightly boiling water. Break each egg into a cup first, then slide into the water. When the water is starting to just bubble, turn the heat as low as possible, cover the pan and leave for a few minutes until set. Lift the eggs out with a slotted spoon into flat bowls, ladle soup around them and sprinkle with coriander, black pepper and salt on the egg, if you like. Serve immediately with chouriço, presunto and bread cubes in the bowl or alongside. *Serves 4*

PURSLANE SOUP

2 TABLESPOONS OLIVE OIL · 1 TABLESPOON BUTTER · 1 LARGE ONION, *roughly chopped* ·
1 CARROT, *peeled and chopped* · 40 G (1½ OZ) CHOURICO OR SPICY SAUSAGE, *cut into 2–3 slices* ·
2 GARLIC CLOVES, *roughly chopped* · 3 TABLESPOONS WHITE WINE ·
600 G (1 LB 5 OZ) POTATOES, *peeled and halved* · 2-3 TEASPOONS COARSE SALT ·
85 G (3 OZ/*heaped* ⅓ CUP) *PARBOILED VARIETY OF* RICE · 125 G (4½ OZ) PURSLANE (*or watercress*) *leaves* ·
½ TEASPOON GROUND CINNAMON · *juice of half a* LEMON · 10 *FRESH* MINT LEAVES, *to serve*

My friend Peta remembers this from her summers in Portugal. The big pot of mixed soup would be on the stove and, while it was boiling, Margarita would come in with bunches of wild leaves collected from the river bank. I loved the shape of the leaves drifting in this soup, and I liked the unfamiliar taste. For a deeper flavour here, use home-made chicken stock instead of water (like this, we have mixed two Portuguese soups into one, taking the mint and lemon that is usually in chicken canja).

Heat the oil and butter in a large stockpot and sauté the onion until softened and golden. Add the carrot and chouriço and sauté for a while longer until it smells good, then add the garlic and cook until you can smell it.

Add the wine and cook until almost evaporated. Add the potato, salt and a couple of twists of pepper, turning it through with a wooden spoon and sautéing for a couple of minutes more. Add 1.5 litres (52 fl oz/6 cups) of hot water. Bring to the boil, lower the heat slightly, cover the pot and cook at a high simmer for 20 minutes or so. Remove from the heat.

With a slotted spoon, scoop out the potatoes into a bowl. Take out the chouriço slices (you can eat them while you work). Purée the rest of the pot, which won't seem much but will, funnily enough, take a while to purée until smooth. Mash the potatoes roughly in the bowl and leave on one side for now.

Add the rice to the pot and bring back to the boil, stirring with a wooden spoon to make sure it doesn't stick. Cover the pot and simmer for 10 minutes. Add the purslane or watercress and mashed potatoes, bring back to the boil, then simmer uncovered for another 10 minutes or so until the rice is just cooked. (Not too soft as it will carry on cooking in the pot until you serve.) Stir the thickened soup every now and then to make sure it is not sticking. Stir in the cinnamon, to taste, and the lemon juice. Serve hot, with mint leaves on top.

Makes about 1.75 litres (61 fl oz/7 cups)

CALDO VERDE

— potato and cabbage soup with chouriço —

2 TABLESPOONS OLIVE OIL • 2 RED ONIONS, *chopped* •
2 GARLIC CLOVES, *chopped* • 700 G (1 LB 9 OZ) POTATOES, *peeled and cut into chunks* •
2 BAY LEAVES • 200 G (7 OZ) *DARK* CABBAGE, *stems removed, very thinly sliced* •
60 G (2 OZ) CHOURICO SAUSAGE • PIRI PIRI OIL OR SAUCE, *for drizzling*

This must be the culinary equivalent of the Portuguese flag and could be a meal in itself with bread. A small bowlful is perfect as a first course if you've got the barbecue going for something else afterwards (the Portuguese do seem to serve up soup as their 'vegetable' and then just meat and potatoes for the main). You can use any dark cabbage — couve, cavolo nero, kale or even savoy — but trim away the thick stems, roll up the leaves into a cigar and slice very very thinly.

Heat the oil in a wide pan and sauté the onions, stirring often because there isn't much oil, until soft and sticky. Add the garlic and potato chunks, stirring while they cook until you start to smell the garlic. Add 1.25 litres (44 fl oz/5 cups) of water and the bay leaves and bring to the boil. Season with a good heaped teaspoon of salt, lower the heat slightly, cover the pan and simmer for 20 minutes or so, until the potatoes are cooked but not soggy. Remove from the heat.

Meanwhile, bring a large pot of salted water to the boil, add the cabbage and simmer for 10 minutes.

With a slotted spoon, remove 2 spoonfuls of potato from the pan and keep on one side. (And discard the bay leaves.) Purée the rest of the soup until completely smooth and then return to the heat. Use your slotted spoon to add the cabbage to the puréed soup, together with about a cupful of its cooking water (or however much you think it needs).

Let it simmer for 5 minutes or so and then add the unpuréed potato near the end so that everything mingles. Check the seasoning, turn off the heat and cover the pan while you prepare the chouriço.

You need your barbecue or chargrill pan to be hot as hot. Cook the chouriço until it's golden and charred here and there, then cut into slices. Ladle the soup into bowls and top each with a few slices of sausage. Add a drizzle of piri piri oil or sauce for some heat, if you like. *Makes over 1.5 litres (52 fl oz/6 cups)*

61

E favor
fecharauporta

...powder - peeled
4 onions whole halved/...... in s...
4 peppers (2 red 2 green)
3 bay lea...
pinch of ...
salt
oil - ...
...
...Benia
...a mullet
...kate
...ntain ... to cook...
...g ...a ...

~ Mains ~
AND SIDE PLATES

Albertina

CALDEIRADA A PORTUGUESA
— *Portuguese fish stew* —

2 OR 3 x 500 G (1 LB 2 OZ) *DIFFERENT WHOLE* FISH. *cleaned and gutted* ·
500 G (1 LB 2 OZ) FISH FILLETS · 4 TABLESPOONS OLIVE OIL ·
1 LARGE ONION. *thinly sliced* · 1 *small* GREEN PEPPER (*CAPSICUM*). *seeded and cut into strips* ·
1 *SMALL* RED PEPPER (*CAPSICUM*). *seeded and cut into strips* · 3 - 4 GARLIC CLOVES. *chopped* ·
5 *LARGE VERY RIPE* TOMATOES. *peeled and thickly sliced* · 1 TEASPOON PAPRIKA ·
2 *pinches of ground* PIRI PIRI · 600 G (1 LB 5 OZ) POTATOES. *peeled and thickly sliced* ·
2 *fresh* BAY LEAVES · 1 *thin* BUNCH OF CORIANDER (*CILANTRO*) · 1 *thin bunch of* PARSLEY ·
125 ML (4 FL OZ/½ CUP) WHITE WINE · PIRI PIRI OIL. *to serve*

I ate this for the first time in a restaurant in Belém, Lisbon. When I asked what was in it, out came Albertina with her head scarf and all her separate bowls of red and green pepper and onion trimmings and cuttings. And, of course, being the character she was, she insisted that I leave with her small recipe book on bacalhau.

This is the sort of rustic fish stew you can imagine being made over a fire on the beach in the early evening by a fisherman, with his wife cutting her vegetables directly into the pot. Some of the fish are cooked on the bone, for wonderful flavour. For the whole fish you could use snapper, hake, whiting, bream, mullet, flathead or flounder. For the fillets, try monkfish, halibut, swordfish, perch or mackerel. Ask your fishmonger to cut off the heads, clean, gut and scale the fish for you and, if you don't like the idea of just throwing out the heads, you can make a quick broth with some carrots, onion and celery to freeze and use elsewhere.

Pat the fish dry with kitchen paper and cut up the large fish into two or three big chunks. Leave the fillets whole.

Heat the olive oil in a large wide pot and sauté the onion until softened and gold. Add the peppers and cook until they soften a bit and start to colour. Add the garlic and, when you can smell it, add the tomatoes. Cook until broken down and pulpy but still in soft chunks. Season with the paprika, piri piri, salt and just a dash of pepper. Add the potatoes and turn well in the sauce.

Cover the pot and cook for 15 minutes or so, until a fork just pierces the potatoes (they mustn't be too soft). Remove half the mixture to a bowl. Put a bay leaf, the parsley and the coriander into the pot and then layer the fish on top and sprinkle with a little salt. Then tip the bowl of tomato, onion, potato mixture back into the pot over the fish.

Add the other bay leaf, pour in the wine and bring back to a gentle boil. Cover and just simmer for 15 minutes, shifting gently with a wooden spoon if necessary to stop anything sticking. Cook until the potatoes and fish are cooked but not falling apart. Add a touch more water if you would like it to have more broth. Keep the lid on and leave to sit for 10 minutes or so before serving. (This is not bad at room temperature either.)

To serve, gently lift out the fish first (remember exactly how many pieces you put in so you know what to look for), getting rid of the bones and skin as much as you can without breaking up the fish.

Ladle the potatoes, vegetables and a good spoonful of broth into bowls and then add the fish. Serve with some piri piri oil, black pepper and bread, and a bowl for any stray fish bones.

Serves 4–6

Straying somehow from a beautiful Algarve beach, we landed upon a Sardine Festival. My kind of fun. Down the endless aisles of homemade cakes and sweets and finally reaching the star of the show — the grill to collect your sardines. We sat at a long wooden bench, between octopus feijoada and sponge cakes, gazing out to sea. There is not a Portuguese in sight who doesn't know how to eat a grilled sardine on bread.

lulas

SQUID CALDEIRADA

1 KG (2 LB 4 OZ) SQUID · 5 TABLESPOONS OLIVE OIL · 2 LARGE ONIONS, _sliced_ ·
1 _large green_ PEPPER (_CAPSICUM_), _seeded and sliced_ · 2 BAY LEAVES · 3 GARLIC CLOVES, _crushed_ ·
A _pinch of ground_ PIRI PIRI · 125 ML (4 FL OZ/½ CUP) WHITE WINE ·
1 TABLESPOON WHITE VINEGAR · 2 TEASPOONS TOMATO PASTE ·
2 TABLESPOONS _chopped_ PARSLEY · 750 G (1 LB 10 OZ) _new_ POTATOES, _peeled and halved if large_ ·
5 _LARGE RIPE_ TOMATOES, _peeled and sliced_

This is Natasha's aunt Helen's recipe — she's an excellent Mozambique-born cook. I baked this in the oven in my big black cast-iron pot — very simple and very good. You could also make it on the stovetop in exactly the same way, covering the pot and simmering over medium heat for 30–40 minutes.

To prepare the squid, firmly pull the head and innards from the body and wash the body. Cut off the head just below the eyes and discard, leaving the tentacles in one piece if they're small. Pull the clear quill out of the body and rinse the tube. Peel off the outer membrane and slice the tube into 3 cm (1 inch) rings.

Preheat the oven to 200°C (400°F/ Gas 6). Heat the oil in a large pan and sauté the onions, pepper and bay until soft. Add the garlic and piri piri and season well. Cook until you can smell the garlic, then add the wine, vinegar and tomato paste and bubble it all up until a bit caramelly. Stir in the parsley.

Layer the ingredients in your pot: some onion and garlic, then potatoes, tomatoes and squid. Then a final onion layer. Season again. Cover and bake for 30 minutes, then give the pot a shake and spoon up some of the juices to baste the top. Cook for 30 minutes more until the squid is tender and the potatoes cooked. Serve with bread and green beans. _Serves 4–6_

sardinhas

GRILLED SARDINES

12 SARDINES, *cleaned and gutted but heads left on* ▪
COARSE SALT ▪ OLIVE OIL ▪ LEMON HALVES, *to serve*

Everywhere in Portugal are sardines… people grilling them, people eating them. This is a treat and fantastic with roasted green peppers and onions and boiled or squashed potatoes. In Portugal it is often served with a corn bread. The sardines must be very very fresh. Portuguese sardines are larger, fatter, meatier and more succulent than those I generally find in Italy. The ones we had were about 18 cm (7 inches) long — just plain, traditional, grilled and delicious with lemon juice and black pepper. The Portuguese generally leave them ungutted, but I like mine cleaned — you can decide which you prefer on your plate. This is a rough guide but, of course, just grill as many as you need.

Heat up your barbecue. Rinse the sardines well and pat dry. Put them in a colander with a gentle sprinkling of coarse salt and leave for 30 minutes. Heat up your barbecue. Splash the sardines with a little oil, scatter with more salt and grill over hot coals for 3 minutes or so on each side until they have firmed up and have good chargrill marks (important for the taste).

Serve hot with black pepper, lemon halves and maybe extra coarse salt. Serve with roasted green peppers with onions and potatoes. *Serves 4*

pimentão

ROASTED GREEN PEPPERS WITH ONIONS

250 G (9 OZ) *small mild green* PEPPERS (CAPSICUMS) • 2 TABLESPOONS OLIVE OIL •
1 *small white* ONION, *thinly sliced into rings* • 1 GARLIC CLOVE, *peeled but left whole* •
1 BAY LEAF • 1 TABLESPOON WHITE WINE VINEGAR • A *sprinkling of* PAPRIKA

These are good with the grilled sardines, any fish grill, or as a salad with a handful of boiled shredded salt cod and some olives mixed in. I got 13 small peppers for my 250 g. If you can't find the small ones (which look lovely whole) then use larger peppers and quarter them. You will probably want to peel the skin off the larger ones. You can add many more peppers to this without increasing the oil and vinegar amounts by much — just taste to see.

Preheat the oven to 200°C (400°F/Gas 6). Rinse your peppers and pat dry with kitchen paper. Roast the peppers on a tray lined with lightly oiled foil for about 15 minutes. Turn them once, taking care not to pierce the skin or the juices will leak out. They shouldn't be too dark — just with blackened roasty parts here and there. Leave to cool.

Heat the oil in a small pan and sauté the onion rings, garlic and bay leaf with a little salt and pepper until softened and just lightly touched with gold. Add the vinegar and paprika and let it bubble up for a few moments. Allow to cool, then pour over the peppers. Scatter with a little more coarse salt and turn everything carefully so the peppers keep their shape. Cover the bowl until you're ready to serve, or keep them in the fridge for up to a day.

Serves 4–6

Lisbon

CHICKEN WITH PEAS

5 TABLESPOONS OLIVE OIL · 1 *LARGE* ONION, *chopped* · 1 CELERY STALK, *chopped* ·
1 CARROT, *peeled and chopped* · 2 BAY LEAVES · 30 G (1 OZ) CHOURICO SAUSAGE, *thinly sliced* ·
60 G (2 OZ) *UNSMOKED* BACON *or pancetta in one thickish slice* · 2 TABLESPOONS *chopped* PARSLEY ·
1 CHICKEN, *skinned and cut up into 10–12 pieces* · 250 ML (9 FL OZ/1 CUP) WHITE WINE ·
3 TABLESPOONS *roughly chopped* TINNED TOMATOES (*or 1 large very ripe tomato, peeled and chopped*) ·
600 G (1 LB 5 OZ) PEAS, *fresh or thawed frozen*

This is an easy, one-pot dish that you can make beforehand, turn off the heat and serve when you're ready. I chop the onion, celery and carrot roughly in a mixer, but not too small please. This is lovely with baked butter rice (page 105) or plain boiled potatoes.

Heat the olive oil in a large non-stick frying pan. Add the onion, celery, carrot and bay leaves and sauté until the onion is golden. Add the chouriço and bacon and cook for a bit longer. Add the parsley and chicken and sauté for a good few minutes until the chicken too is golden. Turn now and then so that nothing sticks and burns. Season with salt and pepper.

Add the wine and let it bubble up for a minute or two, then stir in the tomato. Tip out into a large heavy casserole dish (because later on the peas won't all fit in the frying pan), cover and simmer for 30 minutes on low heat.

Take the lid off, add the peas, turn up the heat a bit and cook for another 10 minutes or so until the peas are just tender and still green. There will still be some liquid in the dish. Taste for seasoning, turn off the heat and leave uncovered (the peas will still be absorbing some of the liquid) until you serve, with bread, potatoes, rice, or whatever you like. *Serves 4–6*

churrasqueira

GRILLED CHICKEN PIRI PIRI

2 X 800 G (1 LB 12 OZ) CHICKENS · 1 LEMON · 3-4 GARLIC CLOVES, *finely chopped* ·
1 TEASPOON DRIED OREGANO · 1 TEASPOON PAPRIKA · COARSE SALT

PIRI PIRI BASTING SAUCE: 6-8 *small dried* PIRI PIRI CHILLIES (OR 3-4 FRESH) ·
3 GARLIC CLOVES, *roughly chopped* · 70 G (2½ OZ) BUTTER · 2 TABLESPOONS OLIVE OIL ·
1 TEASPOON FINE SALT · *JUICE OF* 1 LEMON · 1 BAY LEAF · 2 TABLESPOONS RUBY PORT ·
2 TABLESPOONS WHISKY · *extra ground* PIRI PIRI, *if you like*

This is fantastic. I made it in the Algarve with the wonderful cook Teresa, who I was lucky to find. Thank you, Teresa! It's important to use small chickens or they will have burnt on the outside before they've cooked through. If yours are on the larger side, make sure you slash the flesh well so they cook through.

If necessary, you can make one of the chickens child-friendly by not brushing with the piri piri but, instead, basting it with the lemon garlic marinade while it cooks. The piri piri will strengthen as it sits, so make it fiery enough for your own tastes.

Rinse the chickens and pat dry. Cut each chicken in half so you have four pieces (you can butterfly them, but smaller pieces are easier to cook). Cut off the wing tips and cut a little way into the bone joints so they crack open and flatten to help the chicken cook evenly. Make a couple of slashes where the meat is thickest to be sure that it cooks all the way through.

To make the marinade, cut the lemon in half and squeeze the juice into a bowl that will fit the chickens. Throw in the lemon halves, garlic, oregano, paprika and then the chickens, scattering generously with coarse salt. Turn it all together well and massage into the chickens.

Leave covered (but not in the fridge) for at least half an hour until the chicken has taken in the salt (if you're leaving it longer you'll need to put it in the fridge). Heat the barbecue with a grill 15 cm (6 inches) from the hot coals.

To make the basting sauce, pulse the chillies and garlic to a rough paste in a food processor (or use a mortar and pestle). Heat the butter and oil with the paste in a small pan until it is sizzling and you start to smell the garlic. Add the salt, lemon juice, bay leaf, port and whisky and let it bubble up for 5 minutes, then remove from the heat. Taste and add more ground piri piri if you like.

Shake the chickens out of the marinade and place, skin side up, on the grill. (If the fat drips and causes flames, remove the rack and extinguish the fire with ash or water, otherwise the skin will burn and taste terrible.)

Turn the chickens when the first side is cooked. After 25 minutes or so, when they're almost ready, start basting with the piri piri. Baste a couple of times on each side. Cut each chicken half into four (it's nicer to serve this way and you can check that the bits closer to the bone are cooked) and drizzle with the rest of the piri piri sauce. Serve with tomato rice or chips and salad. *Serves 4*

TOMATO RICE

4 TABLESPOONS OLIVE OIL · 1 *LARGE* ONION, *finely chopped* ·
1 *SMALL RED* PEPPER (*CAPSICUM*), *seeded and finely chopped* · 2 GARLIC CLOVES, *chopped* ·
4 TABLESPOONS *chopped* PARSLEY · 1 *small fresh* BAY LEAF ·
4 *VERY RIPE* TOMATOES, *peeled and chopped (or 400 g/14 oz tin chopped tomatoes)* ·
1 TEASPOON SWEET PAPRIKA · 20 G (³/₄ OZ) BUTTER · COARSE SALT ·
400 G (14 OZ/2 CUPS) *MEDIUM-GRAIN* RICE

This is a kind of 'everywhere' dish, found on the plate alongside grilled prawns, flattened chickens or grilled fish. So it's not usually meant to be in the leading role, but it's very good all the same. You could make it the star by adding a few more vegetables such as celery, zucchini (courgettes) and carrots, all chopped up and cooked with the onion until sticky.

Or add a tablespoon of chopped rosemary, or another herb, with the tomatoes at the beginning for a different flavour. And you could serve it drizzled with piri piri oil. If you don't have lovely ripe tomatoes, then tinned will be better than not-quite-ripe-enough.

Heat the oil in a large frying pan and sauté the onion until sticky and golden. Add the pepper and cook until everything is jammy and turning golden. Add the garlic, parsley and bay leaf and, when you start to smell the garlic, add the tomatoes, paprika, butter, about 2 teaspoons of coarse salt and a little pepper. Simmer for about 5 minutes, mashing up the tomatoes a bit but still leaving a few chunks.

Add the rice and turn it through well to mix in the flavours. Add 1 litre (35 fl oz/ 4 cups) of water, bring to the boil and then simmer for about 10 minutes, checking that nothing is sticking. Turn off the heat and fluff the rice, cover and leave for 10 minutes before you serve. Fluff it through again — it should've absorbed most of the liquid and be just right, in which case serve immediately. If it's too firm, leave it covered for a while longer. Best hot, but also good at room temperature. *Serves 4–6*

BAKED BUTTER RICE

50 G (1¾ OZ) BUTTER · 1 TABLESPOON OLIVE OIL · 1 *SMALL* ONION, *finely chopped* ·
2 *dried* BAY LEAVES · 250 G (9 OZ/1¼ CUPS) *parboiled variety of* RICE · 2 GARLIC CLOVES, *chopped* ·
2 *PINCHES OF* PAPRIKA · 1 LITRE (35 FL OZ/4 CUPS) VEGETABLE STOCK

This can be dressed up or down as much as you like, but I love this stress-free baked rice. You can put it in the oven and go out for a walk, unlike the more usual stovetop rice that needs a touch more vigilance. It's lovely with anything that calls for white rice: chicken with peas, *cozido*, grilled chicken, tomato chilli prawns and so on. You can easily add some extra bits to take on the flavour of the meal — some fresh coriander chopped in at the end, chilli or whatever.

You can use a good stock cube or make a simple vegetable stock by simmering a peeled onion, carrot, celery stalk and seasoning in about 4 cupfuls of water for a while.

Preheat the oven to 180°C (350°F/ Gas 4). Heat the butter and oil in a flameproof casserole (I use my cast-iron one) and sauté the onion with the bay leaves until softened and sticky. Add the rice, garlic and paprika and stir the rice well so it soaks up all the flavours.

Add the stock and season, if necessary. Bring to the boil, then cover with a lid and put in the oven. Cook for 40–45 minutes until all the liquid has been absorbed and the rice is cooked. Take out of the oven and leave for a few minutes before fluffing with a fork to serve. *Serves 4–6*

PORK WITH CLAMS

650 G (1 LB 7 OZ) *SMALL* CLAMS *in shells* · 4 TABLESPOONS OLIVE OIL ·
600 G (1 LB 5 OZ) PORK SHOULDER, *trimmed of excess fat and cut into 3–4 cm (1¹/₂ inch) cubes* ·
1 ONION, *chopped* · 3 GARLIC CLOVES, *chopped* · 125 ML (4 FL OZ/¹/₂ CUP) WHITE WINE ·
JUICE *of half a* LEMON · 500 G (1 LB 2 OZ) POTATOES, *peeled and cubed* ·
2 HEAPED TABLESPOONS *chopped* CORIANDER (*CILANTRO*)

I was a little hesitant about this dish when I first came across it, but it turned out to be one of my favourites. You can also marinate the meat in a little *massa de pimentos* (page 17) before frying, which will change the flavour. Pork fillet is often used here but I love the softness of the pork shoulder after the long cooking time, even if it's not the most traditional cut of meat. If you do use fillet it will need a shorter cooking time, to just brown it. The clams can be steamed separately and then the two united, so that you don't toughen up the meat. Your clams will probably have been purged of sand already but check with your fishmonger, otherwise you'll need to soak them for a day in a colander standing in a bowl of well-salted water, changing the water several times. And if you're at all worried that your clams might still be harbouring some sand, even after you've purged them, steam them in a separate pan. I like to cook it all in one big pot though, for that lovely mingling of flavours. The squares of fried potato are an important part of this dish for mopping up the juices afterwards, so make sure you have them cooked and ready at the same time as your pork and clams.

If you've been soaking your clams, give them a good swirl in the water, rinse them, drain and leave in the colander.

Heat the oil in a large wide pan and add the pork. Sauté over high heat until golden and a bit crusty on both sides (be patient here, because a good deep colour is what will give wonderful flavour to the finished dish).

Season with salt and pepper and add the onion. Continue to sauté until the onion is soft and golden, then add the garlic and cook until you start to smell it. Add the wine and let it bubble up and thicken slightly.

Add 375 ml (13 fl oz/1¹/₂ cups) of water, put the lid on the pan and simmer over low heat for about 1¹/₄ hours, turning the meat a couple of times. If necessary, add a little more water — there should be some slightly thickened sauce in the pan.

Add the clams and lemon juice and season with salt and pepper. Turn the heat up high, put the lid on and cook for 10 minutes or so until the clam shells open. If they haven't all opened, put the lid back on for a couple of minutes and give them another chance, then discard any that are still stubbornly closed.

Meanwhile, parboil the potatoes for 5 minutes in boiling water, drain well and dry with kitchen paper. Fry in plenty of olive oil until crisp, sprinkle with coarse salt and serve immediately. Check the seasoning of the pork and clams, stir in the coriander and take to the table. It can keep for a bit, with the lid on, before serving. *Serves 4*

ROAST LAMB WITH ONIONS AND GREEN PEPPER

1 *smallish* LEG OF LAMB (*about 1.2 kg/2 lb 12 oz or so*) *with bone* · 125 ML (4 FL OZ/½ CUP) OLIVE OIL · 1 TEASPOON PAPRIKA · COARSE SALT · 4–5 SPRING ONIONS (*SCALLIONS*), *trimmed* · 1 LARGE ONION, *quartered* · 4 GARLIC CLOVES, *peeled but left whole* · 4 BAY LEAVES · 600 G (1 LB 5 OZ) POTATOES, *peeled and cut up quite small* · 250 ML (9 FL OZ/1 CUP) WHITE WINE · 1 GREEN PEPPER (*CAPSICUM*), *chopped* · 1–2 TABLESPOONS *chopped* PARSLEY

When you take this out of the oven, tilt the pan so the lovely gravy runs down and is not all absorbed by the potatoes. That way you'll have some pan juices to serve with the roast.

Preheat your oven to 200°C (400°F/Gas 6). Rinse the lamb well and cut away some of the excess fat. Put the oil in a large roasting tin. Put the lamb in the tin and pat all over with the oil and paprika. Season well with coarse salt and pepper. Roast for about 30 minutes until golden on top.

Reduce the oven to 180°C (350°F/ Gas 4). Turn the lamb and add the spring onions, onion, garlic and bay leaves around and under it. Roast for another 30 minutes.

Meanwhile, boil the potatoes in salted water for 10 minutes until just tender. Drain.

Add the wine to the roasting tin and arrange the potatoes, green pepper and parsley around the meat, shuffling them in the juices. Sprinkle the potatoes and pepper with salt.

Roast for 45 minutes or until the potatoes have absorbed some of the juices and are golden, and the lamb is well cooked with a crisp skin. Shuffle the vegetables halfway through the cooking time. Rest the lamb for 10 minutes before carving. *Serves 4–6*

Alentejo

ROAST RABBIT

1.5 KG (3 LB 5 OZ) RABBIT, *WITH LIVER AND KIDNEYS IF POSSIBLE, skinned, cut up into 14 pieces* ·
2 ONIONS, *quartered* · 4 BAY LEAVES · 6 CLOVES · 5 GARLIC CLOVES, *peeled but left whole* ·
125 ML (4 FL OZ/½ CUP) OLIVE OIL · COARSE SALT · 2 TABLESPOONS AGUARDENTE *or brandy* ·
250 ML (9 FL OZ/1 CUP) WHITE WINE · 20–30 G (1 OZ) BUTTER

You can use one or two small rabbits here (you need about 1.5 kg in total). Ask your butcher for the liver and kidneys as well and roast them alongside. They won't take as long to cook, so take them out first and serve as a lovely small appetiser for two, mashed on a piece of grilled bread, while you are waiting for the rabbit to finish cooking. You can make this with chicken as well, but reduce the time by about 15 minutes so it remains succulent.

I ate this in Alentejo, Portugal's inland of endless plains, wheat fields and cork trees, and it is lovely with some sautéed greens.

Put the rabbit pieces in a bowl with any liver and kidneys. Add the onions, bay, cloves, garlic and half the oil. Season and massage it in well. Add the aguardente and wine, cover with plastic wrap and leave to marinate for an hour or so.

Preheat your oven to 200°C (400°F/ Gas 6). Dribble the rest of the oil into a baking dish which will fit the rabbit snugly in a single layer. Lift the rabbit out of the marinade and into the dish. Roast for 30 minutes, turning once, until golden brown, then add all the marinade. Lower the heat to 180°C (350°F/ Gas 4), cover with foil and carry on roasting for 30 minutes or so until tender. Remove the foil, dot with butter and roast for 30 minutes or so until lovely and brown. Add a few spoonfuls of water during the last 30 minutes if it is not looking saucy enough. Serve warm. *Serves 4*

peixe

PAN-FRIED FISH WITH VINEGAR

2 BABY FISH (EACH ABOUT 300 G/10 OZ), *cleaned, gutted and scaled* ·
A *LITTLE* FLOUR · 125 ML (4 FL OZ/½ CUP) OLIVE OIL · COARSE SALT ·
2 GARLIC CLOVES, *peeled and squashed a bit* · 2 BAY LEAVES ·
2½ TABLESPOONS *chopped fresh* ROSEMARY LEAVES ·
125 ML (4 FL OZ/½ CUP) WHITE WINE VINEGAR

My friend Corinne taught me this dish and it's a beauty. It's quick but a bit delicate to make — you need to have your fish cooked just right and simultaneously make sure that nothing burns. So get everything ready before you start. You need nice round, plumpish baby fish here. I used orata (bream) but use anything that will fit in your pan — snapper, flathead, bass, mackerel, haddock… Ask your fishmonger to gut, scale and trim away the fins.

Pat the fish dry, salt well, then pat in flour on both sides. Heat the oil in a frying pan large enough to hold both fish. When hot, add the fish and cook for a few minutes over high heat until golden underneath. Turn over and salt.

Add the garlic and bay and throw in almost half the rosemary. Cook again until the fish is golden underneath. Turn over carefully, taking care not to break the fish, and salt the new topside. The heat should still be high, so sit the garlic and bay on top of the fish if necessary. Add the vinegar and let it bubble for 5 minutes or so until thickened a little. Add the rest of the rosemary and some black pepper and spoon the liquid over the fish a few times. There should be lots of sauce for serving and the fish will be cooked through.

Take the whole pan to the table (with a plate for the bones). The rosemary garlic oil is delicious scraped from the bottom of the pan with chips or bread. *Serves 2*

ROAST OCTOPUS IN
RED WINE WITH POTATOES

500-600 G (ABOUT 1 LB 4 OZ) OCTOPUS · 5 TABLESPOONS OLIVE OIL · 1 ONION, *chopped* ·
2-3 GARLIC CLOVES, *chopped* · 2-3 HEAPED TABLESPOONS *chopped* PARSLEY ·
400 G (14 OZ) TIN *chopped* TOMATOES · *A pinch of ground* PIRI PIRI ·
600 G (1 LB 5 OZ) POTATOES, *peeled and cut into largish chunks* · 185 ML (6 FL OZ/3/4 CUP) RED WINE

This deep and wonderfully flavoured dish was one of the most stunning things I saw in the Azores and I wanted to make it as soon as I got home. Some bread for the leftover sauce is fundamental. The last half an hour of cooking is vital — the octopus needs to soften in the oven first, then roast until it is a bit crusty. Don't take it out too early when it looks still like a boiled dish.

To clean the octopus, cut between the head and tentacles, just below the eyes. Grasp the body and push the beak up and out through the centre of the tentacles with your finger. Cut the eyes from the head. To clean the head, carefully slit through one side, avoiding the ink sac, and scrape out any gut. Rinse under running water to remove any grit. Cut the head into thick slices and the tentacles into 6 cm (about 2 inch) longish pieces on the diagonal.

Preheat your oven to 200°C (400°F/ Gas 6). Heat the oil in a non-stick pan. Sauté the onion until sticky, add the garlic and cook until you can smell it. Add the parsley, sauté for a moment and add the tomato. Season well, add the piri piri and let it bubble up. Simmer for a couple of minutes, squashing down the tomato lumps, then remove from the heat.

Put the octopus and potatoes in a 28 x 18 cm (11 x 7 inch) oven dish that will fit everything in one layer quite compactly. Scrape the tomato mixture over it. Pour in the wine, shuffle everything, and season with salt. Cover with foil and cook for nearly an hour or until the octopus is tender and the potatoes are nicely cooked if you poke a fork into one.

Remove the foil, turn the oven down to 180°C (350°F/Gas 4) and cook for 30 minutes or more until the top is deep roasty-looking here and there, and there is an abundance of almost jammy-looking sauce. Serve with lots of bread for that sauce. *Serves 4–6*

PAN-FRIED LIVER SCHNITZELS
WITH ONIONS

300 G (10½ OZ) CALF LIVER (*or lamb or pork liver, if you prefer*) · 1 LEMON, HALVED, *plus extra to serve* ·
3 GARLIC CLOVES, *1 finely chopped, 2 peeled but left whole* · ABOUT 125 ML (4 FL OZ/½ CUP) OLIVE OIL ·
1 LARGE ONION, *thinly sliced* · 3 BAY LEAVES · ABOUT ½ CUP *dried* BREADCRUMBS

Fried liver, *'iscas'*, was always a regular in traditional old Lisbon taverns.

Wash the liver in cold water, pat dry and cut away any sinew. Slice into 2–3 mm thick pieces (I cut up the longer pieces and ended up with five or six schnitzels). Put the liver in a non-metallic bowl, cover with the juice of one lemon half, the chopped garlic and pepper. Mix well and leave for 30 minutes to 2 hours. (Pork liver can be left for longer.)

Heat 5 tablespoons of the oil in a large non-stick frying pan and sauté the onion with a little salt and pepper until sticky and deep golden, adding a bay leaf towards the end. Tip the pan, holding the onion at the top with your wooden spoon so that the oil runs to one side. Scrape the onion onto a plate, leaving the oil in the pan.

Put the breadcrumbs on a plate. Remove the liver from the marinade and pat in the crumbs on both sides. Add another couple of tablespoons of oil to the pan to cover the bottom. Heat up, then add the liver, whole garlic cloves and remaining bay leaves and sprinkle with a little salt.

When the underside of the liver is golden and crusty, turn over with tongs, sprinkling a little salt on the done side. Fry until the underside is golden and crisp and the liver is cooked through but soft as butter inside. If the garlic is burning, sit it on top of the liver.

Squeeze the juice from the other lemon half all around and scrape the onion over the liver. Put the lid on and let it all bubble for a minute. Turn off the heat and leave for a couple of minutes before serving with lots of black pepper and extra lemon halves for those who love lemon. *Serves 2*

ESPETADA

— beef kebabs with bay leaves —

ABOUT 900 G (2 LB) BEEF FILLET, *WITH SOME FAT ON*, *cut into 5 cm (2 inch) pieces* ·
3/4 TEASPOON GROUND SWEET PAPRIKA · ABOUT 20 *or more FRESH* BAY LEAVES ·
4 GARLIC CLOVES, *peeled and squashed a bit* · 3 TABLESPOONS OLIVE OIL ·
COARSE SALT · 30 G (1 OZ) BUTTER

These spiced grilled skewers are made with many different meats — chicken, fish, lamb — but the one I loved most was fillet. You might like to spice it up a bit with some crushed herbs in the marinade. It's important to use fresh rather than dried bay leaves — they give a wonderful deep and special flavour. You'll need six or so metal or wooden skewers to make these, but when you serve it's not necessary for everyone to have their own skewer: it will depend on how large you cut the pieces of meat. I like this with roasted new potatoes and tomatoes (overleaf).

Put the meat in a bowl and sprinkle with the paprika. Add 2 whole bay leaves, 3 squashed garlic cloves, the olive oil, some pepper and coarse salt. Turn it all through, massaging the salt into the meat. Cover, refrigerate and leave for a couple of hours. If you're using wooden skewers, put them to soak now, so they don't scorch on the barbecue.

Heat up your barbecue and, while it's warming, thread the meat and bay leaves alternately onto skewers. Brush the bay leaves with a touch of oil to stop them burning. Put a rack fairly close over the hot barbecue (about 10 cm/4 inches away) and cook the skewers, turning often, until crusty golden and charred here and there but rosy inside.

Meanwhile, heat the butter with the last garlic clove in a small pan until it's a bit golden and smells good. Keep warm on the side of the barbecue if the skewers aren't yet ready.

Put the skewers on a platter, scatter immediately with a little more coarse salt and pepper, drizzle with the warm butter and serve at once. The meat will be deliciously soft and tender and the juices will seep out and mingle with the butter. *Makes 6 or 7 'big piece' skewers*

vinho verde

ROASTED NEW POTATOES
WITH TOMATOES AND WHITE WINE

60 G (2 OZ) BUTTER, *CHOPPED* · 600 G (1 LB 5 OZ) NEW POTATOES, *peeled and cut in half* ·
1 SMALL ONION, *halved and thinly sliced* · 3 TABLESPOONS WHITE WINE · 1 BAY LEAF ·
2 TABLESPOONS OLIVE OIL · 3 RIPE TOMATOES, *sliced about 1 cm (¹/₂ inch) thick*

This is good with any main course — roast lamb, or a chicken or fish dish — and beautiful with the grilled pork chops (page 135). Use a dish that will fit the potatoes fairly snugly (mine was 18 x 27 cm/7 x 11 inches) in a single layer. You can easily make more than this; just add a little more butter and olive oil, too.

Heat your oven to 200°C (400°F/Gas 6). Scatter pieces of butter here and there over the bottom of your dish and put the new potatoes and onion in the dish. Season with salt and pepper, then add the wine and bay leaf and mix through well. Drizzle with the oil, cover with foil and put in the oven for about 30 minutes until the potatoes are soft.

Take off the foil, turn through again and put back in the oven for about 20 minutes or until the potatoes are looking roasted. Add the tomatoes with an extra sprinkling of salt and pepper and roast for another 15 minutes or longer, or until the tomatoes and potatoes are golden here and there and there's a little gooey liquid in the bottom of the dish. Serve warm, or cover with a cloth if you won't be serving at once. These are still good once they've cooled down. *Serves 4–6*

the hunt

PARTRIDGE AND CABBAGE IN BRANDY

2 *tender young* PARTRIDGES, *plucked and dressed* · FLOUR, *to sprinkle* ·
1 TABLESPOON OLIVE OIL · 85 G (3 OZ) BUTTER ·
300 G (10½ OZ) NEW POTATOES, *peeled and halved* · 1 LARGE ONION, *chopped* ·
1 CELERY STALK, *chopped* · 100 G (3½ OZ) PRESUNTO *OR PROSCUITTO, finely chopped* ·
2 BAY LEAVES · 3 GARLIC CLOVES, *chopped* ·
A *pinch of ground* PIRI PIRI · 250 G (9 OZ) CABBAGE, *thickly shredded* ·
3 TABLESPOONS BRANDY · 2 CARROTS, *peeled and cut into large chunks* ·
125 ML (4 FL OZ/½ CUP) VEGETABLE STOCK · 125 ML (4 FL OZ/½ CUP) WHITE WINE

This makes me think of noblemen on Portuguese carracks laden with spices, sailing back to their homeland and feasting on roast game birds. I love the idea that it is so ancient sounding. You can also make this with poussin (baby chickens), pheasant, pigeon or quails. Use any variety of cabbage you like — green or red, kale, savoy, Portuguese couve, or cavolo nero for its colour is nice too. Use a good stock cube or make a simple vegetable stock by simmering a peeled onion, carrot, celery stalk and seasoning in about 4 cupfuls of water.

Preheat the oven to 180°C (350°F/Gas 4). Wash the birds in cold water and pat dry with kitchen paper, removing any stray feathers. Cut the partridges in half lengthways. Lightly season them, then sprinkle with a little flour.

Heat the oil and half the butter in a large frying pan. When foaming, add the partridge and brown all over. Remove to a plate. Add the potatoes to the pan and toss them until they are a bit crusty. Remove them to the plate, add the rest of the butter to the pan and sauté the onion until turning golden. Add the celery, presunto and bay leaves and cook until they begin to colour. Add the garlic, piri piri and seasoning and cook until you can smell the garlic. Add the cabbage, pour in the brandy, cover and cook for a few minutes to soften the cabbage a bit.

Tip the cabbage mixture into your large cast-iron pot or casserole dish. Push the partridge halves, breast side down, into the cabbage so they are half buried. Tuck the potatoes and carrots around. Pour the stock and wine over the top. Put on the lid and cook for 50 minutes or so until the potatoes and carrots are cooked through.

Increase the oven to 200°C (400°F/ Gas 6). Shuffle the pot a bit to make sure nothing is sticking and add a touch more stock or water if needed. Turn the partridge halves, leave the pot uncovered and cook for a further 15 minutes or so, basting a few times, until the partridge is very tender and crisped but not dry.

Serves 4

Today for lunch on the day that Popsi is leaving, we go to Santa Marta and have the best prego rolls. I ask how they are made... sirloin, grilled. Great tender meat, slightly rosy inside and hanging out of the side of the bread. Seasoned only with salt and put onto their fabulous Portuguese rolls which seem to have a touch of wholewheat flour. Very lightly toasted but not enough to take away from their softness and hurt your palate. I put a little more salt in, a good squeeze of lemon and a splash of the orangey piri piri oil.
I love the soggy first layer of bread.

San Miguel

BAKED PORK RIBS WITH ORANGE

1 KG (2 LB 4 OZ) SHORT PORK RIBS · 125 ML (4 FL OZ/½ CUP) OLIVE OIL ·
2 BAY LEAVES · 125 ML (4 FL OZ/½ CUP) WHITE WINE ·
JUICE OF 1 ORANGE, *PLUS 2 ORANGES, QUARTERED* · 1 *LARGE WHITE* ONION, *chopped* ·
3 GARLIC CLOVES, *chopped* · 3 TABLESPOONS *tinned crushed* TOMATOES ·
2 TABLESPOONS MASSA DE PIMENTOS (*page 17*) · A *pinch of ground* PIRI PIRI, *if you like*

I ate this one night in Ponte Delgada on the island of San Miguel. I asked the chef and this is more or less the recipe he gave me. I was very happy to come home and make it. This makes a big dish of ribs but you just bang it in the oven and it's a lovely, easy way to feed a crowd. If you want to make less, just reduce the amount of ribs, or you could make them all anyway and have leftovers for the next day.

Preheat your oven to 180°C (350°F/Gas 4). Cut the pork ribs into single ribs and trim off excess fat (you should get about 16 ribs). Heat 3 tablespoons of the oil in a large non-stick frying pan and cook the ribs until well browned on the undersides. Turn and cook until deep golden all over (do this in batches if necessary).

Add the bay leaves at the end, season and add the wine and orange juice. Let it bubble away for a few minutes, then turn off the heat.

Meanwhile, heat the remaining olive oil in a small frying pan and sauté the onion until beautifully golden. Add the garlic and, when you start to smell it, add the tomato. Bubble up for a moment, stir in the *massa de pimentos* and piri piri and turn off the heat.

Find a roasting tin that will fit everything snugly in one layer. Put an orange quarter in each corner and dot the rest here and there. Arrange the ribs in one layer and scrape the tomato mixture over them, turning through the ribs and even over the orange quarters. Roast for about 30 minutes until tender and golden and dotted with bits of sauce. Serve hot. *Serves 6*

feijão

GREEN BEANS WITH POTATOES

3 TABLESPOONS OLIVE OIL · 1 *WHITE* ONION, *chopped* · 4 GARLIC CLOVES, *chopped* ·
1 TABLESPOON *chopped* PARSLEY · 1-2 BAY LEAVES · 350 G (12 OZ) *large flat* GREEN BEANS, *topped* ·
750 G (1 LB 10 OZ) POTATOES, *peeled and cut into large chunks* ·
20 G (³/₄ OZ) BUTTER · 250 ML (9 FL OZ/1 CUP) VEGETABLE STOCK ·
A *few dried wild* OREGANO *or* MARJORAM FLOWERS, *if you have some*

This is a very plain and beautiful side dish. I like to leave the beans long and dramatic, but you can cut them shorter for practicality, or use string beans if you can't find the large flat ones. Peel and chop your potatoes beforehand but keep them in a bowl of cold water so they don't darken. You can use a good stock cube or make a simple vegetable stock by simmering a peeled onion, carrot, celery and seasoning in 4 cups of water for a while. If you have some dried oregano or marjoram flowers, scatter them over at the end, but if you don't, just use another chopped herb that you like.

Heat the olive oil in a wide pot and sauté the onion until golden. Add the garlic, parsley and bay leaves and then, when you can smell the garlic, add the whole beans and potatoes. Turn it all through and season with salt and pepper, then add the butter and enough stock to just about cover the beans and potatoes.

Bring to the boil over high heat, then lower the heat slightly, cover and cook for about 20 minutes or until the potatoes are nicely soft but haven't broken up.

Turn off the heat but leave the lid on so that it carries on getting softer until you eat it. This shouldn't be soupy, but a lovely, soft, thick side dish.

Taste for seasoning and scatter with some of the dried flowers or any other herb that you like. *Serves 4–6*

PORK WITH PICKLES
AND POTATOES

500 G (1 LB 2 OZ) *LARGE NEW* POTATOES, *scrubbed but not peeled* · 5 TABLESPOONS OLIVE OIL ·
500 G (1 LB 2 OZ) PORK SHOULDER, *cut into 2–3 cm (1 inch) cubes* ·
1 SMALL ONION, *chopped* · 3 GARLIC CLOVES, *chopped* · 2 BAY LEAVES ·
1 TEASPOON SWEET PAPRIKA · 185 ML (6 FL OZ/3/4 CUP) WHITE WINE ·
20 G (3/4 OZ) BUTTER · 2 TABLESPOONS *chopped* PARSLEY ·
120 G (4 OZ) PICKLES · PIRI PIRI SAUCE OR OIL, *to serve*

Make sure you love the pickles on their own before you put them on top of your pork and potatoes. It's good if there's some chilli in the pickles, but if not you can add a splash of piri piri sauce. I had pork with pickles a few times in Portugal — once, this dish; once, grilled *linguiça* with chopped pickles; and, another time, baked suckling pig with pickles.

Slice your potatoes into 1.5–2 cm (3/4 inch) rounds and then halve or quarter those depending on how big the potatoes were to start with. Bring a pot of salted water to the boil and cook the potatoes until they are just starting to soften (do not overcook here — just to the point where a sharp knife will go through them). Drain and set aside for now.

Meanwhile, heat 3 tablespoons of the olive oil in a large non-stick frying pan and trim the pork of any very excess fat. Fry the meat over high heat, turning it when the undersides are browned. Fry until very deep golden and crispy, then add salt to the meat.

Push the meat to one side of the pan, add the onion and fry over high heat until golden. Add the garlic, bay, paprika and some pepper. Take care not to burn the garlic.

Add the wine and leave it all to bubble up, then lower the heat. Add about 125 ml (4 fl oz/1/2 cup) of water, put the lid on the pan and simmer over low heat for almost an hour (adding a little more water later if necessary) until the sauce is glossy and fairly reduced. The meat should be lovely and tender. Check the seasoning and keep the pan covered while you cook the potatoes.

In another non-stick frying pan, heat the remaining oil and the butter until fizzling. Add the potatoes in a single layer and sauté until the bottoms have a lovely crust. Turn them over and when they're almost done, mix in the parsley, shake some paprika over the top and taste for seasoning.

Serve the pork with potatoes on top and some pickles on top of them. Add a dash of piri piri sauce if you feel like it. *Serves 4*

leitão

ROAST LEG OF
BABY PORK

1 x 2.25 KG (5 LB) _leg of baby_ PORK · 7 GARLIC CLOVES, _peeled_ · 4 TABLESPOONS OLIVE OIL ·
JUICE _of half a_ LEMON · 1 _heaped_ TEASPOON MASSA DE PIMENTOS (_page 17_) ·
1 TEASPOON TOMATO PASTE · $^1/_4$ TEASPOON _ground_ PIRI PIRI · 3 _fresh_ BAY LEAVES ·
3 TEASPOONS COARSE SALT · 250 ML (9 FL OZ/1 CUP) WHITE WINE ·
2-3 TABLESPOONS AGUARDENTE _OR BRANDY_ · 2 _LARGE_ ONIONS, _quartered_

It is very common to find slow-roasted suckling pig in Portugal. Many times I tasted the pork of the wonderful _pata negra_, a black-hoofed pig that feeds off acorns. When I ate roast pork in a restaurant they told me that they don't cook it themselves — there is a special oven some-where and everyone sends out for their bit. This is crispy outside, but so soft inside. You can even roast it slowly overnight.

This is a lesser portion, using leg instead (you can easily make a whole suckling pig too, just cook it for longer). And, if you'd like to make your own Portuguese _bifanas_, you can fill bread rolls with warm slices of pork, ladle a little gravy in too and a sprinkling of piri piri. This is even very nice the next day with some quince marmalade (page 226) melted into sauce. But I liked this best with the pork migas (overleaf).

With a sharp knife, make slashes across the skin of the pork a couple of centimetres (1 inch) apart. Here and there, make a cut about 1 cm ($^1/_2$ inch) deep and stuff in one of the whole garlic cloves until you have used four of them.

Heat the oven to 220°C (425°F/Gas 7). Purée the remaining garlic in a mincer or chop up until almost a paste. Mix in 2 tablespoons oil, the lemon juice, _massa de pimentos_, tomato paste and piri piri. Put the bay leaves in a large roasting tin and put the pork on top, skin side up. Pour the marinade all over the pork.

Turn the pork over and sprinkle with a teaspoon of salt and some pepper. Massage into the skin, then turn skin side up again and sprinkle with the rest of the salt and more pepper. Drizzle the remaining oil over and under the pork and add 125 ml (4 fl oz/½ cup) water to the tin. Cover with a large sheet of foil lined with a sheet of baking paper so the foil doesn't stick.

Roast for 30 minutes, then turn the oven down to 120°C (235°F/Gas ½), pour in the wine and aguardente and cover again. Roast very slowly for another 4½–5 hours, adding the onions for the last hour, until the pork is very tender and cooked through.

Remove the foil and turn the oven right up again to 200°C (400°F/Gas 6) and spoon some pan juice over the meat. Roast for another hour or so until the top is deep golden and crisp and the sauce is deep golden too, bubbling up and a bit thickened. Don't let the tin dry out: check occasionally and add more water if needed. (If you like the skin even crisper, you can take the pork out of the tin and onto a tray and continue crisping it in the very hot oven for a further 20 minutes or so.)

Leave to rest for, say, 20 minutes, before cutting the pork into chunks or slices. Serve with the pan gravy, onion wedges and pork migas (right). *Serves 6–8*

PORK MIGAS

125 ML (4 FL OZ/½ CUP) OLIVE OIL · 1 *SMALL* ONION, *chopped* ·
240 G (9 OZ) CHOURICO SAUSAGE, *chopped* ·
60 G (2 OZ) *thick unsmoked* BACON *OR PANCETTA, chopped* ·
1 OR 2 *pinches of* PAPRIKA · 2 BAY LEAVES · 2 GARLIC CLOVES, *chopped* ·
2 TABLESPOONS *chopped* PARSLEY · 50 G (1¾ OZ) BLACK OLIVES, *chopped* ·
200 G (7 OZ) *YESTERDAY'S COUNTRY-STYLE* BREAD, *torn into bits* ·
500 ML (17 FL OZ/2 CUPS) HOT VEGETABLE STOCK

Migas is a very tasty dish of bread cooked in the pan where you have just fried sausages, pork or the such like, so that the bread picks up all the flavours and juices from the pan. For elegance, you can quenelle or shape the migas and bake it again for a short while in a very hot oven to crisp it up. Really, I prefer to just serve it warm in lovely rich dollops, rather like mashed potato, which is how it was served to me in Alentejo. The wonderful bread of Alentejo would, of course, be the best to use here, but any country-style bread such as ciabatta will do. Use a good stock cube or make a simple stock by simmering an onion, carrot, celery stalk and seasoning in 4 cupfuls of water for a while.

Heat the oil in a large, deep non-stick frying pan. Sauté the onion, chouriço, bacon, paprika and bay leaves until golden and sticky. Add the garlic, parsley and olives and sauté for another minute or so until you can smell the garlic. Add the bread and sauté until it has soaked up all the flavoured oil, the pan is dry and the bread starts to look a bit toasted.

Add the stock and let it all bubble up, mashing the bread in with your wooden spoon. Leave to simmer until all the liquid has been absorbed and the bread is starting to look dry. Taste for seasoning and serve immediately with roast pork. *Serves 6–8 (with roast pork)*

churrasco

GRILLED PORK CHOPS WITH CHOURICO AND PANCETTA

6 *fresh* BAY LEAVES, *torn in half* • 4–6 *good-sized* PORK CHOPS (*depending on how many you are*) •
1 HEAPED TEASPOON COARSE SALT, *plus extra for serving* •
3 *large* GARLIC CLOVES, *peeled and sliced* • 125 ML (4 FL OZ/½ CUP) WHITE WINE •
3 TABLESPOONS OLIVE OIL • 4–6 SLICES *rindless* PANCETTA, *1 cm (½ inch) or so thick* •
1 *WHOLE* CHOURICO SAUSAGE • A LEMON, *for serving*

I love this with squashed potatoes (overleaf) but you could serve with roast or boiled. Tomato rice (page 104)) is also good. You could use other cuts of pork here or shuffle things around to suit your taste.

Put 3 of the bay leaves in a large dish and arrange half the chops over the top. Sprinkle the chops with some of the salt, the rest of the bay leaves and the garlic. Put the remaining chops on top, pour the wine and olive oil over them, scatter with the rest of the salt and turn it all in the marinade. Cover and leave for a couple of hours, turning a couple of times. Add the pancetta to the marinade.

Heat up a chargrill pan or barbecue grill,

put the chops on the grill and place a garlic slice and bay leaf over each one for flavour. Grill for a few minutes on each side (depending on their thickness), basting often, until the chops are cooked through and have deep golden ridges here and there. They should be lovely and charred, but not overcooked.

Slash the chouriço a few times and add to the grill. Then add the pancetta, which is thinner and will only take a couple of minutes to cook. Turn them so they heat through and are golden charred here and there.

Serve hot with a sprinkling of coarse salt and perhaps a drop of olive oil. Cut the chouriço into thick slices and squeeze a little lemon juice over it. *Serves 4–6*

squashed

BATATAS A MURRO
— squashed potatoes —

about 1 KG (2 LB 4 OZ) NEW POTATOES, *unpeeled* · OLIVE OIL, TO COAT ·
4 *fresh* BAY LEAVES · 6 PEPPERCORNS · A *pinch of* PAPRIKA ·
A *pinch of ground* PIRI PIRI · 4 *HEAPED* TEASPOONS COARSE SALT

These go anywhere and with anything. You can use smaller or larger new potatoes and add any herbs or flavourings such as lemon rind to the salt, but in Portugal it was usually just the lovely simple coarse salt. If you're feeling lazy you can roll all the potatoes in the spiced salt and maybe have a double layer of foil ready to wrap them all together rather than in their own little parcels. And if you're doing them in salt only, you don't have to wrap them at all — just roast and bash.

Heat your oven to 200°C (400°F/Gas 6). Rinse and pat dry the potatoes, then put in a bowl and drizzle with olive oil, turning them so they're well coated. Cut the middle stems from the bay leaves and tear the leaves into pieces, then grind with the peppercorns, paprika, piri piri and half the salt in a spice mill or mortar and pestle until you have a dry-looking powder.

Tear sheets of foil large enough to wrap each potato. Put the spice powder on a plate and mix with the remaining salt. Roll the potatoes in the spiced salt (not every millimetre has to be covered), wrap in foil and put straight on the oven rack. Bake for 45 minutes to an hour or until the potatoes are cooked through. Open the foil and give each potato one frustration-banishing crack with your palm to just open them but not to squash them flat.

Serve drizzled with the olive oil left in the foil parcels, adding more if you like. *Serves 4–6*

Lisbon

COFFEE STEAK

1 TABLESPOON BUTTER • 1 TABLESPOON OLIVE OIL •
1 X 150 G (5½ OZ) FILLET STEAK, *about 2 cm (¾ inch) thick* • COARSE SALT •
2 BAY LEAVES • 2 GARLIC CLOVES, *unpeeled* • 1 TABLESPOON CREAM •
about 2½ TABLESPOONS *strong* ESPRESSO COFFEE

Lisbon is a society of steak-lovers and this is just one of the many ways it is served. Daniela told me about this first, and then I ate it at a *cervejaria* in Lisbon. Although it sounds a bit rich, it's just right. There is just about enough sauce here for two steaks, if you want. You pour the steak and sauce all onto a plate, so you don't even have to go to the bar for a coffee afterwards! I loved it for the very idea.

Heat a blob of the butter with the oil in a non-stick frying pan that will hold your steak compactly. When it starts to fizzle, add the steak and cook until golden. Turn over and sprinkle with coarse salt. Cook until the steak is done to your liking (I like mine to be deep charred and crusty on the outside, but still rosy inside). Add the rest of the butter towards the end of the cooking, turn the steak again and sprinkle with coarse salt. Add the bay leaves and garlic to the pan to flavour the sauce and lift the steak out onto a plate.

Add the cream and coffee to the pan and let it bubble up to thicken for a few seconds. Turn off the heat and return the steak to the pan, then leave for a minute to let the juices mingle. Grind a lot of black pepper over the top once it's on the plate. Excellent with chips for dipping in the sauce.

Serves 1

BITOQUE STEAK
WITH EGG

1 TABLESPOON OLIVE OIL, *plus a little extra for the egg* ·
180 G (6 OZ) RUMP STEAK, *about 1 cm (¹/₂ inch) thick, see below* · COARSE SALT ·
2 GARLIC CLOVES, *crushed* · 1 BAY LEAF · 1 TABLESPOON BUTTER ·
1 *scant* TEASPOON SWEET PAPRIKA · 3 TABLESPOONS WHITE WINE ·
¹/₈ TEASPOON FLOUR · 1 EGG · PIRI PIRI SAUCE, *to serve*

In Portugal this is what I often ate, served in its individual earthenware dish. Your steak should be about 1 cm (¹/₂ inch) thick and very tender. I like to have the one large steak on my plate so I buy a 2 cm (³/₄ inch) thick rump steak (about 180 g/6 oz or so) and slice horizontally almost all the way along, then open it out, butterflied. Perfect. If you prefer to see smaller pieces of meat on your plate, two 90 g (3 oz) steaks would work just as well. You can also add some piri piri in with the paprika from the beginning or splash piri piri sauce over as you are eating. Serve this with chips or sautéed potatoes for dipping in the egg and perhaps crisp-fried thin onion rings on top.

Heat the oil in a non-stick frying pan and, when it is very hot, sear the steak well on one side. Turn the steak, salt the seared side and add the garlic and bay leaf to the pan. Cook over very high heat until the steak is deeply seared. Turn over and salt the other side.

Add the butter and paprika to the pan, swirling it around and scraping up any crusty bits. Sit the garlic on top of the steak if it looks like burning. When the butter is golden, lift the steak out onto a plate and cover loosely with foil. Add the wine to the pan and let it bubble up. Scatter the lightest dusting of flour into the pan and whisk so there are no lumps. When the sauce has reduced and thickened a bit, taste for seasoning. If the sauce is too thick, add a drop of water and let it bubble up again. You need a lot of sauce here, so don't reduce it too much.

Meanwhile, drizzle a tiny bit of oil into your smallest non-stick saucepan and heat it up. Break the egg into the pan, sprinkle some salt on top and let it cook until the white is just turning a bit brown and frayed at the edges. Put a lid on to finish cooking the egg until there is a thin film of white over the yolk but it is still runny and bright yellow.

Place the egg on top of the steak and pour a generous amount of sauce around your plate. Grind black pepper on the egg and serve with piri piri sauce. *Serves 1*

Azores

STEAK REGIONAL

250 G (9 OZ) RUMP STEAK, ABOUT 2 CM (³/₄ INCH) THICK *
1 TABLESPOON BUTTER * 1 OR 2 BAY LEAVES * COARSE SALT *
2 GARLIC CLOVES, *peeled and squashed a bit* * 2 *pieces* AZOREAN RED PEPPERS (*page 16*), *rinsed* *
2 TABLESPOONS BRANDY OR WHISKY * PIRI PIRI OIL, *to serve* * LEMON HALVES, *to serve*

This is a very popular way to serve steak on the island of San Miguel in the Azores. I loved their special peppers that were often added in whole chunks to dishes at the end of the cooking, and the millions of blue-lilac hydrangeas to be seen everywhere in August. This also works well as a petisco plate: slice up the cooked meat, leave out the peppers and serve with little forks or toothpicks.

Trim the steak of excess fat and slice it horizontally to get two 1 cm (¹/₂ inch) thick pieces or, if you prefer a thicker steak, leave it whole. Heat the butter over your highest heat in a non-stick frying pan that will just fit the meat snugly. When the butter is fizzling, add the steak to the hot pan with the bay leaves and cook until the underside is deep golden. Turn over and sprinkle with coarse salt. Add the garlic and cook until the other side of the meat is deep golden, adding the peppers towards the end of the cooking.

Pour in the brandy or whisky and ignite (take care as it will flame high) and cook for just a few seconds more until there is some dark sauce in the pan (if it seems as if the butter is close to burning at any point, add an extra blob to slow it down).

Remove from the heat and leave to rest for a moment. Serve drizzled with some piri piri oil and a squeeze of lemon.

Serves 1–2

prego prego

PREGO ROLLS

2 X 120 G (4 OZ) RUMP OR SIRLOIN STEAKS, *about 5 mm (¼ inch) thick* •
3 TABLESPOONS RED WINE • 2 *fresh* BAY LEAVES • 2 GARLIC CLOVES, *peeled and squashed a bit* •
30 G (1 OZ) BUTTER • 1–2 TABLESPOONS OLIVE OIL, *for frying* •
2 PORTUGUESE BREAD ROLLS • PIRI PIRI SAUCE, *to serve*

☘ I would have gone to Portugal just for these. I would follow people through alleyways to find the best ones. So enthusiastic am I for prego rolls that I'm including two different ways to make them. Dress this up with a beautiful bottle of red and a tablecloth, or dress it down with a couple of beers (and no tablecloth). Your meat must be thin and top quality such as rump or sirloin, about 120 g (4 oz) per person (unless you're particularly hungry and want both rolls yourself). These are perfect when the meat is deep seared on the outside and rosy inside. It's important that the bread is warm and soft — I love that first layer that is soggy from the juices of the meat and yet still a bit crusty. I would wish a Portuguese baker for

every neighbourhood, but if you don't have Portuguese bread rolls, use similar floury soft ones.

↝

Marinate the steaks in the wine, bay leaves and one of the garlic cloves for a couple of hours before you cook them.

Heat the butter with the other garlic clove in a small pan until the butter turns a bit golden. Season lightly with salt and pepper.

Shake the meat out of its marinade and pat dry with kitchen paper. Heat the olive oil over high heat in a non-stick pan that will fit the steaks. When the pan is very hot, add the meat and fry very quickly, turning once. Remove to a plate, keep warm and add a dash of salt to the meat while it's resting. Meanwhile, put the halved rolls under the grill until very slightly crisp and warm.

Pour the meat marinade into the pan and let it bubble up well. When it has thickened a bit and tastes good, dip the cut sides of the rolls in to soak up some sauce.

Put the bottom half of the roll on a plate, blob some garlic butter on and then the steak. Pour on any juices from the steaks when they were resting and scatter with salt and a drizzle of piri piri sauce. Put the top on the rolls, squash together and serve at once, with a bottle of piri piri sauce so everyone can do their own thing. Must be eaten warm. *Serves 2 (or 1 very hungry person)*

ANOTHER WAY TO MAKE PREGO ROLLS

OLIVE OIL, *for brushing* · 2 x 120 G (4 OZ) RUMP OR SIRLOIN STEAKS, *about 5 mm ($^1/_4$ inch) thick* · 2 PORTUGUESE ROLLS · BUTTER · COARSE SALT · 1 LEMON · PIRI PIRI SAUCE, *to serve*

You need a barbecue or chargrill pan here for cooking the steaks. I find the piri piri and lemon essential, but you decide.

Heat your barbecue grill plate or chargrill pan and lightly brush with oil. Sear the meat quite deeply, as quickly as you can. Halve the rolls and toast until they are just slightly crisp, then dot with butter. Remove the steaks to a plate, scatter with salt and pepper and leave for a couple of minutes to draw out the juices. Put the meat into the rolls (either cut in half, or left to hang out of the bread) and pour over any juices from the resting meat.

Squeeze some lemon juice over the top and drizzle with as much piri piri as you like (or extra olive oil if your piri piri sauce is quite strong). Squash together and eat warm. *Serves 2*

ervilhas

PEAS WITH EGGS AND CHOURICO

50 G (1¾ OZ) CHOURICO SAUSAGE · 4 TABLESPOONS OLIVE OIL ·
1 SMALL ONION, *finely chopped* · 1 GARLIC CLOVE, *peeled and squashed a bit* ·
1 TABLESPOON *chopped* PARSLEY · 400 G (14 OZ) PEAS, *fresh or thawed frozen* ·
2 EGGS · A *little ground sweet* PAPRIKA

 This looks lovely when you serve the eggs with bright green peas clinging here and there onto their whites. It tastes gorgeous, too, especially if you leave the egg yolk soft and can dip into it with a floury Portuguese bread roll. At Easter this should be made with eggs laid on Good Friday. Use a large frying pan that you can add the eggs to and then take it all to the table. Frozen peas are almost as good as fresh, just defrost them first.

Cut the chouriço into thin slices (removing the casing if it seems thick), then in half again and even into quarters (depending on its original size). Heat the oil in a large non-stick frying pan and sauté the onion until it is golden and sticky. Add the chouriço, garlic clove and parsley and sauté for a few minutes until it looks good, then add the peas and season well.

Mix together so the flavours meld and add a cup of hot water. Simmer over high heat for about 10 minutes, until the peas are soft but still bright green and have just about drunk up all the water. Remove the garlic.

Make two spaces in the peas with a wooden spoon towards the edge, big enough to fit an egg each. Crack the eggs into the holes, sprinkle with a little coarse salt and put a lid on the pan. Cook until there is a thin, pale film over the eggs and the whites are just set with the yolks quite soft. Serve at once with a sprinkling of paprika and pepper if you like. *Serves 2*

meia dose

SALT COD WITH TOMATOES, RED PEPPERS AND OLIVES

ABOUT 350 G (12 OZ) BACALHAU (*SALT COD*), *soaked* · 5 TABLESPOONS OLIVE OIL ·
1 ONION, *halved and thinly sliced* · ½ RED PEPPER (*CAPSICUM*), *roughly chopped* ·
1 GARLIC CLOVE, *chopped* · 1 BAY LEAF · 3 TABLESPOONS WHITE WINE ·
200 G (7 OZ) *tin chopped* TOMATOES · 6 *small new* POTATOES, *peeled* · ABOUT 10 OLIVES

Before you use the salt cod you need to soak it to remove the excess salt. Rinse the cod pieces first, then put them in a large bowl with enough water to completely immerse them. Cover the bowl and refrigerate, changing the water 3–4 times a day. Ask your fishmonger how long you need to soak the cod (it's usually about 2–3 days). If you're unsure, test the cod by breaking off a small fleck, rinsing and tasting it. The tail part is always a bit more salty. In some places you can buy ready-soaked salt cod, which is very reliable and convenient. You could also make this with fresh cod or other fish fillets (without the soaking, of course).

Preheat the oven to 200°C (400°F/Gas 6). Drain the bacalhau well, pat dry with kitchen paper and cut into three or four pieces.

Heat 2 tablespoons of the oil in a frying pan and sauté the onion until softened and turning gold. Add the pepper and cook until golden. Add the garlic and bay leaf and turn through the oil, then add the wine and let it bubble up. Add the tomatoes with about 3 tablespoons of water. Simmer for a few minutes and remove from the heat. Check the seasoning, as you may not need extra salt because of the bacalhau. Scrape the tomato sauce into an oven dish that will fit the bacalhau snugly in a single layer.

Cut the potatoes in half vertically so they are round, or into quarters if they're quite big. Lay the bacalhau over the tomato sauce in a single layer with the potato pieces dotted here and there. Some of the sauce will find its way over the fish and potatoes. Drizzle the rest of the oil over the top. Cover the dish with foil and put in the oven. Bake for about 20 minutes, then take off the foil and cook for another 30 minutes or until the fish and potatoes are cooked and the tomatoes and onions are turning crusty golden here and there. Scatter with olives and cook for another 5 minutes. Sprinkle with parsley to serve, if you like. *Serves 2*

FRIED SALT COD

500 G (1 LB 2 OZ) BACALHAU (*SALT COD*), *soaked* ·
JUICE *of half a* LEMON, *other half cut into wedges to serve* · 2 GARLIC CLOVES, *squashed and roughly chopped* ·
1 BAY LEAF, *torn in half* · A LITTLE FLOUR · OLIVE OIL, *for frying*

I love this with the black-eyed beans (overleaf), which is how I ate it at Casa do Cheias in Ponte de Lima. I found a lovely lady there who I wanted to go and cook with, but she couldn't speak a single word of English, and I couldn't speak a word of Portuguese.

Before you use the salt cod you need to soak it to remove the excess salt. Rinse the cod pieces first, then put them in a large bowl with enough water to completely immerse them. Cover the bowl and refrigerate, changing the water 3–4 times a day. Ask your fishmonger how long you need to soak the cod (it's usually about 2–3 days). If you're unsure, test the cod by breaking off a small fleck, rinsing and tasting it. The tail part is always a bit more salty. In some places you can buy ready-soaked salt cod which is very reliable and convenient.

Drain the bacalhau well and pat dry with kitchen paper. Remove the skin and cut the fish lengthways into three or four pieces. Put in a bowl with the lemon juice, garlic, bay leaf and some pepper. Spoon this over the fish, cover the bowl and leave for at least 30 minutes.

Heat enough olive oil in a small non-

stick pan to come halfway up the side of the fish. Shake the fish from the marinade, pat dry with kitchen paper, then dust with flour on both sides. Add the fish to the hot oil and leave until you're sure it has a deep golden crust underneath (if you fiddle with it, it can flake and collapse all over your pan). Turn very carefully and cook until both sides are lovely deep golden and crisp. Lift out onto a plate lined with more kitchen paper to soak up the oil. Serve hot with lemon wedges and the black-eyed bean salad. *Serves 3–4*

BLACK-EYED BEAN SALAD

500 G (1 LB 2 OZ) *dried* BLACK-EYED BEANS · ABOUT 5 TABLESPOONS OLIVE OIL ·
3 SHALLOTS *OR 1 ONION, chopped* · 1 *small* RED PEPPER (CAPSICUM), *seeded and chopped* ·
1 *small* GREEN PEPPER (CAPSICUM), *seeded and chopped* · 3-4 GARLIC CLOVES, *chopped* ·
4 TABLESPOONS *chopped* PARSLEY · 1 TABLESPOON RED WINE VINEGAR ·
JUICE OF 1 LEMON · *A good pinch of ground* PIRI PIRI

This is the salad that was served as a bed for the fried bacalhau, but it would be delicious with almost anything. If you have leftovers for the next day you might like to moisten the beans with a touch more dressing.

Cover the beans with plenty of water and soak overnight. Drain the beans, put them in a large pot and cover with fresh water. Bring to the boil, skimming off any scum that rises to the top, then lower the heat slightly and cook for about 35 minutes until soft but not mushy. Drain the beans again, then leave to cool in the colander before tipping into a serving bowl.

Heat 2 tablespoons of the oil in a small pan and sauté the shallots until golden. Add the peppers and cook until they are softened and turning golden but not dark. Add the garlic and sauté for 1 minute until you start to smell it, then turn off the heat. Stir in the parsley and add to the beans in the bowl.

Mix together the remaining olive oil, the vinegar, lemon juice and piri piri. Season well with salt and pepper and pour over the bean salad. Toss well before serving.

Serves 4–6

another way

FLAKED SALT COD WITH TOMATO AND ONIONS

450 G (1 LB) BACALHAU (*SALT COD*), *soaked* • 4 TABLESPOONS OLIVE OIL •
400 G (14 OZ) ONIONS, *sliced into rings* • 2 *SMALL FRESH* BAY LEAVES • 4 GARLIC CLOVES, *chopped* •
3 TABLESPOONS WHITE WINE • 200 G (7 OZ) *tin chopped* TOMATOES •
A good pinch of ground PIRI PIRI • *A handful of* CORIANDER (*CILANTRO*) • PIRI PIRI OIL, *to serve*

Before you use the salt cod you need to soak it to remove the excess salt. Rinse the cod pieces first, then put them in a large bowl with enough water to completely immerse them. Cover the bowl and refrigerate, changing the water 3–4 times a day. Ask your fishmonger how long you need to soak the cod (it's usually about 2–3 days). If you're unsure, test the cod by breaking off a small fleck, rinsing and tasting it. The tail part is always a bit more salty. In some places you can buy ready-soaked salt cod, which is very reliable and convenient.

Drain the bacalhau well and pat dry. Remove the skin and bones and break into large flakes.

Heat the oil in a large deep frying pan and sauté the onion with the bay leaves and a dash of salt until golden and sticky. Add the garlic and cook until you start to smell it, then add the wine and cook until it has evaporated.

Add the tomatoes, piri piri and some pepper and cook for about 10 minutes until jammy and smoothish. Add the bacalhau flakes, folding them gently through the mixture. Add 3 tablespoons of water, cover the pan and simmer for 10–15 minutes, until the liquid is drawn out and the flavours develop. Add a little more water if necessary. Taste for seasoning and scatter with coriander and a splash of piri piri oil. Good with rice and green beans. *Serves 4*

BACALHAU COM NATAS

— salt cod with cream and potatoes —

400 G (14 OZ) BACALHAU (*SALT COD*), *soaked* · OLIVE OIL, *for frying* · 2 LARGE ONIONS, *chopped* ·
4 TABLESPOONS WHITE WINE · 2 *pinches of ground* PIRI PIRI · 2 BAY LEAVES

BECHAMEL SAUCE: 40 G (1½ OZ) BUTTER ·
40 G (1½ OZ) PLAIN (*ALL-PURPOSE*) FLOUR · 500 ML (17 FL OZ/2 CUPS) *warm* MILK

950 G (2 LB 2 OZ) POTATOES, *peeled* · 250 ML (9 FL OZ/1 CUP) CREAM ·
ABOUT 1 TABLESPOON FINE BREADCRUMBS

This rich rich gratinéed bacalhau is Daniela's recipe. It is a stunning winter supper — the onions, cream and fried chips join with the salt cod in a delicious sweetness — and lovely served with a dish of green beans. Before you use the salt cod you need to soak it to remove the excess salt. Rinse the cod pieces first, then put them in a large bowl with enough water to completely immerse them. Cover the bowl and refrigerate, changing the water 3–4 times a day. Ask your fishmonger how long you need to soak the cod (it's usually about 2–3 days). If you're unsure, test the cod by breaking off a small fleck, rinsing and tasting it. The tail part is always a bit more salty. In some places you can buy ready-soaked salt cod, which is very reliable and convenient.

Have ready a deep ovenproof dish of about 22 x 30 cm (9 x 12 inches).

Drain the bacalhau and flake into large pieces, discarding the skin and bones. Bring a pan of water to the boil, add the fish and boil for 2 minutes or so (taste a little flake of fish to check it's not still too salty: if so, change the water and boil a little longer). Drain very well.

Heat 4 tablespoons olive oil in a pan and fry the onions until golden and sticky. Add the wine, piri piri, bay leaves and a twist of pepper and simmer for another 5 minutes or so to mingle the flavours. Mix the fish loosely into the onions and remove the bay leaves. Taste for seasoning (you may not need to add extra salt), cover and set aside. Heat your oven to 200°C (400°F/Gas 6).

Make the béchamel sauce. Melt the butter in a saucepan. Whisk in the flour and cook for a few minutes, stirring, then begin adding the warm milk. It will be immediately absorbed, so work quickly, whisking with one hand while slowly pouring milk with the other. When the sauce is smooth and not too stiff, season and continue cooking and stirring for 5 minutes or so, even after it comes to the boil. It should be a very thick and smooth sauce.

Cut up the potatoes into long thin chips and pat dry with kitchen paper. Heat enough olive oil in a large non-stick frying pan to cover the bottom generously. Fry the chips in two batches until golden and crisp here and there. Lift out with a slotted spoon and drain on kitchen paper. Sprinkle lightly with salt.

Dollop half the bacalhau–onion mixture over the base of the dish, then scatter with half of the chips. Repeat the layers again, then spoon the béchamel over the top, tipping the dish from side to side and spreading with a spatula so it's all more or less covered.

Pour the cream over the top and rock the dish a little so it settles in well. Sprinkle with breadcrumbs and bake for about 15 minutes or until nicely golden on top and bubbling here and there. Cool a bit before serving.

Serves 4–6

BACALHAU A GOMES DE SA
— salt cod with potatoes and egg —

500 G (1 LB 2 OZ) BACALHAU (*SALT COD*), *soaked* · 375 ML (13 FL OZ/1½ CUPS) MILK ·
2 BAY LEAVES · 4–5 PEPPERCORNS · 500 G (1 LB 2 OZ) POTATOES, *peeled and thickly sliced* ·
ABOUT 8 TABLESPOONS OLIVE OIL · 2 LARGE ONIONS, *sliced* · A *handful of black* OLIVES, *halved* ·
A *handful of chopped* PARSLEY · 3 *HARD-BOILED* EGGS, *cut into wedges*

This dish is seen everywhere in Portugal in some form or another; this particular version belongs to Natasha's aunt, Helen. It needs to end up with enough sauce to not be dry but, if you prefer, you can use a little less oil. It's best to buy the thick, middle pieces of salt cod and, before you use it, you need to soak it to remove the excess salt. Rinse the cod first, then put in a large bowl with enough water to completely immerse. Cover the bowl and refrigerate, changing the water 3–4 times a day. Ask your fishmonger how long you need to soak the cod (it's usually about 2–3 days). If you're unsure, break off a small fleck, rinse and taste it. The tail part is always a bit more salty. In some places you can buy ready-soaked salt cod which is very reliable and convenient.

Drain your bacalhau, rinse and put in a saucepan. Cover with boiling water, put the lid on and leave to soak for about 20 minutes (taste a flake to check it's not still too salty: if it is, drain and cover with fresh boiling water and leave a while longer). Drain again, remove the skin and bones and flake into large flat pieces.

Heat the milk in a pan with the bay leaves and peppercorns, turning off when it is just coming to the boil. Add the bacalhau to the pan of milk and leave for about 1½–2 hours.

Meanwhile, boil the potatoes for about 10 minutes, until tender but not mushy; drain. Preheat the oven to 200°C (400°F/Gas 6).

Heat 4 tablespoons of the oil in a large frying pan and fry the onions until golden, then add the potatoes. Drain the bacalhau (keeping the milk) and add to the pan, without stirring too much or potatoes and fish will disintegrate. Season with salt, if necessary, and pepper.

Drizzle about 2 tablespoons of oil into a deep 26 cm (10½ inch) oven dish. Put the onions, potatoes and bacalhau in the dish with the olives and parsley. Drizzle here and there with a bit more olive oil.

Pour in about 125 ml (4 fl oz/½ cup) of the milk you saved, rocking the dish so that it soaks into everything. Bake for 10 minutes until golden here and there. Sprinkle with a little more parsley and top with egg wedges. *Serves 4–6*

FRIED TUNA WITH TOMATOES AND ONIONS

ABOUT 5 TABLESPOONS OLIVE OIL · 2 GARLIC CLOVES, *peeled and squashed a little* ·
400 G (14 OZ) *tin chopped* TOMATOES, *OR 4 RIPE TOMATOES, peeled and chopped* ·
2 ONIONS, *thinly sliced* · 3 TABLESPOONS WHITE WINE VINEGAR ·
2 *THICK* TUNA STEAKS, *cut in half* · DRY BREADCRUMBS · *chopped* PARSLEY

This is a dish that is lovely taken directly from your stove to the dining table and served straight from the cooking pot. I like to sit the crusty breadcrumbed chunks of tuna on top of the warm tomato sauce, but if you won't be serving this immediately, keep the tuna on a plate so the crumbs stay crisp, then warm up the sauce for serving at the last minute.

Heat 2 tablespoons of the olive oil in a pan, add the garlic and cook until you start to smell it. Add the tomatoes and season with salt and pepper. Simmer for 5–10 minutes, then add 3 tablespoons of water so your sauce isn't too thick. There should still be some rustic lumps of tomato in it. Take out the garlic, taste for seasoning and set aside with the lid on.

Heat the remaining oil in a large non-stick frying pan and sauté the onions over medium heat. Season and cook until they are soft and golden, turning with a wooden spoon occasionally to make sure none are burning. Add the vinegar and simmer until it is just absorbed. Tilt the pan, keeping the onions to one side with your spoon to drain the oil away from them. Lift out the onions with a slotted spoon and keep warm (you'll use the onion-flavoured oil to cook the tuna).

Rinse the tuna and pat dry with kitchen paper. Put some breadcrumbs on a plate, then coat the tuna in the breadcrumbs. Add a little more oil, if needed, to the pan and place over the heat. When hot, add the tuna and fry until a deep golden crust has formed underneath. Turn over and salt the done side. When the underside is crusty, turn again and salt the top.

Sit the tuna on the tomato sauce in its pot and take to the table. Serve up some onions on the plate, then some tuna and tomato on top of those. Scatter with parsley and serve with crispy fried or boiled potatoes.

Serves 4

lulas

GRILLED SQUID WITH CHOURICO
AND LEMON CORIANDER OIL

600 G (1 LB 5 OZ) BABY SQUID · 150 G (5½ OZ) CHOURICO SAUSAGE ·
2 TABLESPOONS BUTTER · 2 GARLIC CLOVES, *roughly chopped*

LEMON CORIANDER OIL: 1 *handful* CORIANDER (*CILANTRO*) LEAVES · JUICE *of half a lemon* ·
2 TABLESPOONS OLIVE OIL · ½ TEASPOON SALT · 2 *large* ANCHOVY *fillets in oil, drained*

This is a beauty. Sometimes I have bought frozen, cleaned baby squid tubes with tentacles attached — they certainly save preparation time.

I ate grilled squid in many places, the first time in a restaurant on the north coast. I pointed to table three, indicating that I wanted some of the sauce they had. But they are having meat, she mimed. I pantomimed that I'd like to try it anyway and it was fantastic. I had some grilled chouriço on the table and I ate them together. In true Portuguese-style I left the restaurant after a chat in a non-existent common language with the ladies in the kitchen, holding a small glass bottle full of lovely coriander sauce.

If you're using wooden skewers, soak them in water for a while first so they don't scorch.

To prepare the squid, firmly pull the head and innards from the body and wash the body well. Cut off the head just below the eyes, leaving the tentacles in one piece, and discard the head. Pull out the transparent quill, rinse the tube and peel off the outer membrane.

Cut the chouriço into about 8 chunks. Thread the pieces of squid (body and tentacles) and chouriço alternately onto your skewers.

Heat the butter and garlic in a small pan. Sizzle just until the garlic chunks are starting to crisp up but are not yet turning golden. Remove from the heat immediately as the garlic will carry on simmering in the butter as it cools.

To make the lemon coriander oil, pulse half the coriander with the lemon juice, oil, salt and anchovies in a blender until you have chunky flecks of green sauce.

Preheat your grill. Brush the skewers with the garlic butter and grill until charred here and there (probably more noticeable on the chouriço), brushing occasionally with the butter. Take great care not to overcook — the squid must be cooked through but still tender.

Serve the skewers drizzled with the lemon coriander oil. Lovely with boiled potatoes dressed with olive oil.

Serves 2 (or 4 as a starter)

The house here in Carvoeiro is lovely. We have been eating mainly home-cooked meals. Giovanni goes running every morning. Yesterday he came back with handfuls of almonds he'd picked from the trees. Today he arrived with wild thyme stalks. And there is Teresa, the cook and good-at-everything kind of person, who is a dream. She is bustling and jolly with a solution for any problem and a very infectious laugh. When I asked her if she'd like a glass of wine she said, 'Would you like me to sing?'

STUFFED SQUID WITH CHOURICO

12 SQUID, *each about 12 cm (4 inches) long* • 500 G (1 LB 2 OZ) POTATOES, *peeled and cut into chunks* •
125 ML (4 FL OZ/½ CUP) OLIVE OIL • 1 ONION, *finely chopped* •
85 G (3 OZ) CHOURICO SAUSAGE, *very finely chopped* • 85 G (3 OZ) *green or red* PEPPER (*CAPSICUM*), *diced* •
2 *LARGE* GARLIC CLOVES, *chopped* • 3 TABLESPOONS *chopped* PARSLEY •
2 TABLESPOONS RUBY PORT • A *pinch of* PAPRIKA •
2 TOMATOES, *peeled and quartered* • 125 ML (4 FL OZ/½ CUP) WHITE WINE •
dried wild FENNEL *sprigs or flowers, crushed* (*OR 1 TEASPOON CRUSHED SEEDS*) • 2 BAY LEAVES

Squid and cuttlefish (*lulas* and *chocos*) are a popular catch for the fishermen of the Algarve. The wine, oil and stuffing here all work together to keep the squid tender.

To prepare the squid, firmly pull the head and innards from the body and wash the body well. Cut off the head just below the eyes and discard the head. Pull the transparent quill out of the body and rinse out the tube. Peel off the outer membrane, wash and pat dry the squid with kitchen paper. Chop the tentacles finely.

Boil the potatoes in lightly salted water until just cooked. Drain and set aside for now.

Preheat your oven to 180°C (350°F/ Gas 4). Heat 2 tablespoons olive oil in a non-stick pan and sauté the onion until golden. Add the chopped tentacles and sauté until golden, then add the chouriço and pepper and cook until sticky looking. Add the garlic and parsley and cook until you can smell the garlic. Add the port and cook for a few minutes until it reduces a bit. Taste for salt, pepper and paprika. Leave to cool slightly.

Roughly divide up the mixture among your squid, filling each one about two-thirds full and weaving the tops closed with toothpicks. Put into a large oven dish and scatter the potatoes and tomatoes around — the dish should be big enough for it all to fit in one compact layer. Drizzle with 4 or so tablespoons of olive oil and pour in the wine. Season and crush a couple of dried fennel sprigs over the top. Tuck in the bay leaves.

Roast for about 30 minutes or until golden on top. Spoon some pan juices over the top occasionally and give it all a shuffle around. Increase the oven to 200°C (400°F/Gas 6) for another 20–30 minutes until all well roasted and with some thickened juice. *Serves 4*

cerveja

PRAWNS IN BEER

1 KG (2 LB 4 OZ) *large raw* PRAWNS · 100 G (3½ OZ) BUTTER ·
½ TEASPOON SWEET PAPRIKA · *A pinch of ground* PIRI PIRI · 1 TEASPOON COARSE SALT ·
4 GARLIC CLOVES, *roughly chopped* · 185 ML (6 FL OZ/¾ CUP) BEER

I found this at The Radium Beer Hall in Johannesburg and I love it. Thank you to Manuel, and to Artemis for managing to pass the recipe on to me. Manny says to use a good, fairly strong beer with character because that's what will end up on your plate. A couple of tablespoons of cream bubbled in at the end is very good. Or you could take it in an entirely different direction with a squeeze of lemon and a handful of chopped coriander, parsley or even dried basil (as Manny often uses).

Leave the shells on the prawns but cut down the back of each one and devein so they take in the flavour of the sauce. Rinse well. Heat half the butter in a deep frying pan. When it sizzles, add a layer of prawns, pressing them down well so they are butterflied and become golden brown and crisp. If there isn't room for them all in your pan, remove them as they're cooked to make space for the rest. Don't overcook them or they'll lose their succulence.

When all the prawns are cooked, add the paprika, piri piri, salt and black pepper to the pan. Cook for a bit, then add the garlic and the rest of the butter. When you can smell the garlic, remove the prawns to a plate.

Pour the beer into the pan and increase the heat to high so that it bubbles and thickens. Return the prawns to the pan.

Put the lid on and rock the pan from side to side to coat the prawns with hot sauce. Serve with crusty bread or chips to dip in the sauce. And a glass of cold beer... *Serves 4–6*

FISH GRILL WITH LEMON OIL

LEMON OIL: 30 G (1 OZ) BUTTER · 2 GARLIC CLOVES, *chopped* · A *pinch of* PAPRIKA ·
A *pinch of ground* PIRI PIRI · ³/₄ TEASPOON TOMATO PASTE ·
125 ML (4 FL OZ/½ CUP) OLIVE OIL · *juice of* 1 LEMON · 1 TEASPOON *chopped* PARSLEY

big CLAMS *in shells* · 2 X 400 G (14 OZ) *long slim* FISH *such as mackerel, trevally or mullet, cleaned and gutted* ·
2 X 400 G (14 OZ) *plumper* FISH *such as orata (bream), spigola (bass) or snapper, butterflied* ·
1 OR 2 *thick* FISH FILLETS *such as persico (perch), swordfish, snapper, cod or soaked bacalhau (salt cod)* ·
a few SARDINES, *cleaned and gutted* · COARSE SALT ·
LEMON HALVES, *to serve* · *slices of* WHITE *COUNTRY-STYLE* BREAD

This is one of my favourites here — a real Portuguese feast. It sums up everything about the Portuguese table to me. Try to get some good variety in taste and form… a thick fish fillet, a plump fish that you can butterfly and grill opened, some big sardines, even a few clams as I had them in Portugal, simply set on the grill until they opened. A couple of mackerel is also a beauty here. Do as the Portuguese do and use whatever fish are freshest and best on the day. Have your fish all cleaned, gutted, scaled (and fins cut away with scissors) and ready for the barbecue (the fishmonger can do this for you). Your clams will probably have been purged of sand already but check with your fishmonger, otherwise you'll need to soak them for a day in a colander standing in a bowl of well-salted water, changing the water several times. Have your side dishes ready before you put the fish on the grill, and the wine cold, and some *fado* playing…

First make the lemon oil: heat the butter with the garlic, paprika and piri piri until you start to smell the garlic. Remove from the heat and stir in the tomato paste, oil and lemon juice.

Season well, add the parsley, cover and set aside. Have all your serving plates ready.

If you've been soaking your clams, swirl them in the water, rinse, drain and leave in the colander. Heat your barbecue coals. It is best to cook the fish in racks, otherwise place a grill over the coals. Slash the whole fish and brush on both sides with lemon oil, then sprinkle well with coarse salt. Cook the butterflied fish, skin side down, then turn and brush the other side with lemon oil. Cook until nicely charred here and there with cooked white flesh. Sit the clams directly on the rack until they open right up.

Serve the fish immediately, splashed with a little more lemon oil, and lemon halves if you like. Add a few drops of lemon juice to the clams or just eat them as they are, straight from the shells. Grill the bread on both sides and drizzle with a little of the lemon oil. Serve with the fish grill. *Serves 4–6*

For dinner we sat on the river's edge, watching the sky change from day to night and the tide creep in so the couple of boats that were just on sand would be swaying on the water a while later. Our table was wobbling, and I asked the waitress if she had something to put under the leg. So she brought out half a lemon. Ludi and I were shaking with laughter. The next table later got one of those small tubs of sardine paté, upside down. I hope this sleepy Tavira town always stays like this. The lovely water reflections of old, white, sad buildings and now and then a beautiful church, its cross illuminated in emerald green as if for Christmas. When we got the bill, I mentioned that I liked the dish holding our olives. Our waiter immediately picked it up, tossed the remaining olives onto the paper tablecloth, and that was that. 'In the bag' he said to me. So I obeyed and later noticed suspicious looks from table four.

MARINATED BAKED FISH

MARINADE: 1/2 LARGE ONION, *roughly chopped* · 2 GARLIC CLOVES, *peeled and squashed* ·
2 BAY LEAVES · JUICE *of half a* LEMON · 2 TABLESPOONS OLIVE OIL

900 G (2 LB) *thick* FISH *fillets with bone* · 600 G (1 LB 5 OZ) POTATOES, *scrubbed but not peeled* ·
4 TABLESPOONS OLIVE OIL · 4 ONIONS, *thinly sliced* · 1 TABLESPOON TOMATO PULP

This is from Rita, the lovely lady from *Cabo Verde* who lives up the road from me in Italy. She came for dinner and we cooked this together. I asked if all the ladies in *Cabo Verde* are as beautiful as her. 'Oh, much more than I,' she replied, her lovely skin glistening and her almond eyes catching a glint of the afternoon sun as we swung our hips to Cesaria Evora. She looked about 25 but was many years on from there. When we cooked this, we used swordfish, but you could use any thickish fillets on the bone, such as cod, tuna or even soaked bacalhau. And you can use vinegar instead of lemon juice in the marinade if you prefer.

For the marinade, mix together the onion, garlic, bay leaves, lemon juice and oil and season with salt and pepper. Leave the fish to marinate in this for an hour or so.

Boil the potatoes whole in their skins in a large pan of water until soft but not breaking up. Drain well, cool a little and then peel away the skins and slice the potatoes into rounds about 1 cm (1/2 inch) thick. Preheat your oven to 200°C (400°F/Gas 6).

Heat half the oil in a pan and sauté the onions with a little salt and pepper until golden and sticky. Add the tomato pulp and a cupful of water and cook until melted down and soft but with a good amount of sauce.

Lift the fish out of the marinade and into a frying pan over high heat (there's oil in the marinade so you shouldn't need any extra in your pan). Cook the fish until it's browned on both sides, then add the marinade to the pan, reduce the heat a touch and cook until it has thickened a little.

Transfer the fish to a roasting tin in a single layer. Tip the sliced potatoes into the frying pan with the remaining 2 tablespoons of oil and a little salt and turn through the sauce. Tip over the fish.

Spoon the onions over the top of the fish and potatoes and put the tin in the oven for 15–20 minutes, or until nicely roasted but not drying out. *Serves 4*

piri piri

PIRI PIRI AND LEMON BUTTER GRILLED PRAWNS

1 KG (2 LB 4 OZ) *LARGE RAW* PRAWNS

TOMATO PIRI PIRI OIL: 185 ML (6 FL OZ/³⁄₄ CUP) OLIVE OIL · 2 RIPE TOMATOES, *sliced* ·
¹⁄₄ TEASPOON SUGAR · 4 GARLIC CLOVES, *roughly chopped* ·
4 *DRIED* PIRI PIRI CHILLIES *(or other chillies)* · ¹⁄₄ TEASPOON GROUND PIRI PIRI, *if you like*

LEMON BUTTER: 125 G (4¹⁄₂ OZ) BUTTER ·
JUICE OF 1 LEMON · 1 GARLIC CLOVE, *squashed a bit*

I made these with my friend Corinne. She is a truly excellent cook and added this beautiful tomato piri piri oil which is now an almost permanent fixture in my kitchen. That same day, Tina added her rosemary potatoes to the table and it was one of my best meals. So this is how I give it to you. You could also make the prawns plain on a skewer (still in their shells) or butterflied on the grill with a slight drizzle of the tomato piri piri oil, a sprinkling of salt and pepper and a lemon half to serve.

Remove the heads from the prawns if you prefer, but leave the shells on the bodies. Make a shallow cut down the back of each one so they take in the flavour of the sauce, and devein them. Rinse and pat dry.

For the tomato piri piri oil, heat the oil in a smallish saucepan, add the tomatoes and simmer for 20 minutes or so until jammy. Add the sugar, garlic, chillies and some salt and simmer for another 5–10 minutes. Purée until fairly smooth and then taste and see if you'd like the extra piri piri. The oil will strengthen as it sits, so you could make it the day before.

To make the lemon butter, heat the butter and garlic until golden and smelling good. Reduce the heat and whisk in the lemon juice, letting it bubble up. Add salt and pepper and leave to cool. (You can make this beforehand and even set the pan on the side of the barbecue to heat while your prawns are on.)

Heat your barbecue and brush the prawns, inside and out, with the lemon butter. Salt the insides. Try to keep the prawns butterflied as they are grilling so they taste great and cook evenly. Cook until golden underneath and charred a bit here and there (don't over-cook them) then turn over and brush with the butter again. Once the prawns have curled up, sit them on the flesh side so the meat is chargrilled and coloured as well. Paint as often as possible with the lemon butter.

Serve straightaway with any remaining lemon butter drizzled over the prawns while they're still hot. Spoon the tomato piri piri oil over them or on the side and serve with potatoes with olive oil, coarse salt and rosemary or chunky bread. *Serves 4–6*

salt

POTATOES WITH OLIVE OIL, COARSE SALT AND ROSEMARY

ABOUT 1.8 KG (4 LB) NEW POTATOES, *scrubbed and halved if large* ·
2 TABLESPOONS *roughly chopped* ROSEMARY LEAVES *(pulled off a couple of large sprigs)* ·
2 *LARGE RED OR WHITE* ONIONS, *roughly chopped*
2 *heaped* TEASPOONS COARSE SALT · ABOUT 125 ML (4 FL OZ/½ CUP) OLIVE OIL

This I got from my friend Tina, a fun and spontaneous lady, who made it to go with the piri piri prawns at my house one evening. The original recipe was made, I believe, with a couple of bay leaves in the pot but Tina added the rosemary which I truly love. Try to find small new potatoes that can be cooked whole; the skins are left on here. The potatoes must be beautifully cooked (Portugal being such a potato-loving land) and Tina says don't be stingy with the onions. The beauty here is the salt — the coarse crystals like small diamonds scattered onto the potatoes, still with a bit of crunch when you bite them. You'll need a few large sprigs of rosemary: pull the leaves from a couple of sprigs and chop coarsely or snip the leaves directly into the pot. Save the other sprigs for decorating at the end. And use the very best olive oil you can here.

Bring the potatoes, rosemary and onions to the boil in a large unsalted pot of water. Lower the heat slightly and cook for 20 minutes or so until the potatoes are soft but not falling apart and the rosemary is softened.

Drain into a bowl and scatter with the salt, some pepper and olive oil. Mix through gently so the potatoes don't break up too much. You can decorate with a couple of fresh sprigs of rosemary. Lovely warm or cold. *Serves 4–6*

- *The grill on Tavira Island* -

I peered into the kitchen of Il Formosa and a very friendly guy called me in. It was an outside grill with a cover on. They were grilling bream, tuna, sardines, all in racks and I asked if I could watch. Another Portuguese 'yes'! This couldn't have happened in many places. They had a white plastic bucket with a big brush in it and a reddish oil. Oil, lemon and pimento, they said. I looked in the bottom and there was almost a paprika paste. They were doing the sardines in racks — just however many fitted into the rack were scooped out of their big orange bucket of sea water and splattered with coarse salt, then served seven to a portion. No more oil, no more salt, just served nice and charred as they came, and that was that. The other large fish were halved horizontally, opened out onto a rack, brushed, splattered with salt and grilled. Everything is brushed with the same oil, same grill, same brush, said Philippe — a lovely lunatic who was the first to invite me in. He set two clams on the grill and just left them till they opened. He took them off and gave one to me, showing me to pluck out the clam then drink the juice. Delicious: no salt, no oil, just the sea for flavouring. At one point they offered me a beer in the kitchen with a piece of salted eel with a sword nose; an old tradition in the bars of the Algarve. Philippe's been doing this forever, it seems, like a perfect orchestra. Dashing from one side of his grill to the other, twisting and flipping racks over, hopping on one flip-flop as a large grain of hot salt falls off a sardine and onto his foot. He sends sardines off with one hand, flips a rack with the other and shouts an order at the same time. There is a tidy shuffling noise from the *senhoras* in their salad and roast section. They are busy, busy.

MACKEREL WITH SAUCE VILAO
AND SWEET POTATOES

SAUCE VILAO: 1 TABLESPOON BUTTER · 1 GARLIC CLOVE, *peeled and squashed a bit* ·
2 TABLESPOONS BEER · *juice of half a* LEMON ·
1 TABLESPOON OLIVE OIL · 1½ TEASPOONS MASSA DE PIMENTOS *(page 17)*

2 X 240 G (8 OZ) MACKEREL, *cleaned and gutted* · 1 *LARGE* GARLIC CLOVE, *chopped* ·
2 TABLESPOONS *chopped* PARSLEY · 1 TEASPOON *crushed dried* FENNEL *flowers or ground seeds* ·
COARSE SALT · FLOUR, *for dusting* · 1 BAY LEAF ·
2 TABLESPOONS OLIVE OIL · 3 TABLESPOONS WHITE WINE ·
3 TABLESPOONS BEER · 300 G (10½ OZ) SWEET POTATOES, *peeled and cut into 8 chunks* ·
OLIVE OIL OR BUTTER AND SALT, *for serving*

You can also serve this sauce over fried bacalhau or other fish, which is how it was also given to me. Here the mackerel is oven roasted; in the Azores the fish were much smaller (called horse mackerel) and they were deep-fried, but any oily fish will work well with the sauce. You could also use large sardines (just a few more: say 6–8 to make a meal). Or, if you can't get small whole oily fish such as mackerel, you could use one larger (about 500 g/1 lb 2 oz) fish such as trevally or mullet, or fillets. If you use one large fish, you'll need to cook it for about 10 minutes longer. And if you're lighting your barbecue, these are also fantastic on the grill. Stuff them as in the recipe, but leave out the roasting oil.

In the Azores they have nyams with big elephant-ear leaves, growing everywhere around the hot springs, and these appeared in many of the dishes of San Miguel. Orange sweet potatoes work fine here. Serve with cold beer.

Make the Vilão sauce first. Heat the butter and garlic in a small pan until it starts to turn golden, then add the beer and let it bubble up for a couple of minutes. Add the lemon juice and let that bubble up too for a couple of minutes. Add the oil and *massa de pimentos* with some salt and pepper to taste. Let it all bubble up again, then remove from the heat for now (remove the garlic clove and reheat gently later to serve warm).

Heat the oven to 200°C (400°F/Gas 6). Put your fish on a board and make sure they are rinsed and patted dry. Chop or pound together the garlic, parsley and fennel (I crushed them all together to a rough paste in my mortar and pestle). Stuff this into the fish cavities and season the fish skin with salt and pepper. Pat the fish lightly with flour and put, side by side,

into an oven dish with the bay leaf. Drizzle the olive oil under and over.

Bake in the oven for about 10 minutes. Check nothing is sticking and pour in the wine and beer. Cook for another 15–20 minutes, until the fish is cooked through and there is some tasty, roasty-looking sauce.

Meanwhile, boil the sweet potatoes in a large pan of salted water until soft. Drain and drizzle with some olive oil or butter and a little salt. Spoon the warm Vilão sauce over the hot fish on your plate and serve with the sweet potatoes. *Serves 2*

From my terrace perched in the blue Azorean winds of the Atlantic I write. There is a little church in the green garden and hydrangeas everywhere. Black sand. Waterfalls. And the smell of blossoms at night. Cows, rabbits, horses, whales and dolphins — jumping in the way they do to make the whole world love them. Where am I? Ireland? Sri Lanka? This is many places melted into one beautiful harmony.

TRIPE WITH WHITE BEANS

300 G (10½ OZ) *dried* WHITE BEANS, *such as cannellini, soaked overnight* ·
1 LITRE (35 FL OZ/4 CUPS) CHICKEN STOCK · 3 BAY LEAVES ·
750 G (1 LB 10 OZ) HONEYCOMB TRIPE, *bleached and par-cooked* · 1 LEMON, *quartered* ·
4 TABLESPOONS OLIVE OIL · 1 LARGE ONION, *chopped* · 1 CARROT, *peeled and finely chopped* ·
1 CELERY STALK, *chopped* · 85 G (3 OZ) CHOURICO SAUSAGE, *chopped* ·
2 GARLIC CLOVES, *chopped* · A *pinch or two of ground* PIRI PIRI ·
2 TABLESPOONS *chopped* PARSLEY · 1 TABLESPOON RED WINE VINEGAR ·
400 G (14 OZ) *tin chopped* TOMATOES · 125 ML (4 FL OZ/½ CUP) WHITE WINE

Porto, in the north of the country, is so famous for its tripe that its inhabitants are known as *tripeiros*, 'the tripe-eaters'. My history book told that in 1415 the good citizens of Porto salted all their fresh meat and gave it to the navy fleet that was setting sail to capture the Moorish stronghold of Ceuta. They kept only the tripe for themselves.

Ask your butcher whether the tripe needs soaking beforehand. Soak the dried beans in plenty of cold water overnight before you start.

Drain the beans and put in a pan with the stock and one bay leaf. Bring to the boil, then reduce the heat and simmer for 30 minutes until just cooked. Take the pan off the heat but leave the beans in the liquid.

Meanwhile, wash the tripe well, hold it over a bowl and snip with scissors into 2 cm (3/4 inch) wide strips. Squeeze the lemon juice over it, turn through and leave for 30 minutes.

Heat the oil in a large cast-iron pot or casserole and sauté the onion until turning gold. Add the carrot and celery and soften for a few minutes, then add the chouriço, garlic, piri piri, parsley and remaining bay leaves. Let it all bubble away for a bit.

Heat the oven to 200°C (400°F/Gas 6). Drain the tripe, add to the pot and stir to coat. Splash in the vinegar and cook over high heat, stirring often, until the juices have evaporated. Add the tomato, wine and 500 ml (17 fl oz/ 2 cups) of bean cooking liquid (top up with water if needed). Keep the beans on one side.

Season, cover and bake for 30 minutes or so. Reduce the oven to 180°C (350°F/Gas 4), stir in the beans, cover again and bake for another hour or until the tripe is tender. The juice should be thick and rich (add a little extra stock or water if necessary). If the tripe is not tender, carry on cooking until it is (the time will depend on how par-cooked your tripe was to begin with, so taste occasionally). Check the seasoning, scatter with a bit of extra parsley and serve with bread to soak up the lovely juices.

Serves 6

FISH COZIDO

650 G (1 LB 7 OZ) BACALHAU (*SALT COD*), *soaked* • 4 TABLESPOONS OLIVE OIL •
1 ONION, *chopped* • 100 G (3¹⁄₂ OZ) CHOURIÇO SAUSAGE, *chopped* •
1 GREEN PEPPER (*CAPSICUM*), *roughly chopped* • 2 GARLIC CLOVES, *chopped* • 1 TEASPOON PAPRIKA •
A *sprinkling of ground* PIRI PIRI • 2 BAY LEAVES • 400 G (14 OZ) *tin chopped* TOMATOES •
2 TABLESPOONS *chopped* PARSLEY • 1 TABLESPOON MASSA DE PIMENTOS (*page 17*) •
500 G (1 LB 2 OZ) POTATOES, *peeled and thickly sliced* •
300 G (10¹⁄₂ OZ) SWEET POTATOES, *peeled and thickly sliced* • 4 CARROTS, *peeled and cut in half*

§ You can use any firm white fish fillets, such as snapper or fresh cod, here instead of the salt cod. If you do use salt cod, you'll probably need to soak it beforehand to remove the excess salt. Rinse the cod pieces first, then put them in a large bowl with enough water to completely immerse them. Cover the bowl and refrigerate, changing the water 3–4 times a day. Ask your fishmonger how long you need to soak the cod (it's usually about 2–3 days). If you're unsure, test the cod by breaking off a small fleck, rinsing and tasting it. The tail part is always a bit more salty. In some places you can buy ready-soaked salt cod, which is very reliable and convenient. A large, wide cast-iron pot is best for this (mine is 30 cm/12 inches across and 10 cm/4 inches high).

Heat the oven to 180°C (350°F/Gas 4). Drain the bacalhau, pat dry and cut into large serving pieces. Heat the oil in a large cast-iron pot or casserole and sauté the onion until golden and a bit sticky. Add the chouriço and pepper and continue cooking until softened slightly. Add the garlic, paprika, piri piri and bays. When you can smell the garlic, add the tomato and crush a bit with your wooden spoon.

Simmer for a couple of minutes, then season with pepper (you may not need salt here, because of the cod). Remove from the heat. Add the parsley, *massa de pimentos*, bacalhau, potatoes, sweet potatoes and carrots and gently turn through so the sauce is well distributed. Pour in about 125 ml (4 fl oz/¹⁄₂ cup) of water, put on the lid and bake for about 50 minutes.

Use your wooden spoon to check that nothing is sticking, put the lid back on and return to the oven for another 30 minutes or until it is golden and has some nicely bubbling thickened sauce.

The flavours are best here if you have time to leave it for an hour now, with the lid still on, in the switched-off oven. Serve with some bread to soak up the lovely juices. *Serves 4*

COZIDO

450 G (1 LB) *slice of raw unsmoked* PORK BELLY (*PANCETTA*) ·
450 G (1 LB) *slab of* PORK SHOULDER, *about 5 cm (2 inches) thick* ·
450 G (1 LB) CHICKEN *leg and thigh* (*MARYLAND*) *with skin* · 600 G (1 LB 5 OZ) *boneless piece of* BEEF SHIN ·
300 G (10½ OZ) BABY BEETROOT OR TURNIPS, *or both* · *quarter of a small* CABBAGE, *cut into 2 slices* ·
2 *LARGE* CARROTS, *peeled and halved* · 500 G (1 LB 2 OZ) POTATOES, *peeled but left whole* ·
300 G (10½ OZ) *SMALL* SWEET POTATOES, *unpeeled and cut into chunks if large* ·
1 WHOLE CHOURICO SAUSAGE (*about 180 g/6 oz*) · 4 *cabbage chunks (any sort: couve, cavolo nero, kale or savoy)*

I feel this is somehow the culmination of my journey. Traditionally, *cozido à Portuguesa* uses various exotic meats like pigs' ears and blood sausage. I have chosen some more conservative cuts but you may be as traditional as you wish. On the island of San Miguel in the Azores this is called '*cozida à moda das Furnas*' — in the town of Furnas it is cooked in a pot in the earth by the heat of the volcanic lava. It's a spectacular sight. I have used an oven here! You'll need a large cast-iron pot for this (mine is 30 cm/12 inches across and 10 cm/4 inches high) but if your pot is bigger, then even better! Alter the quantities depending on how many will be eating.

Preheat the oven to 200°C (400°F/Gas 6) and cut the pork belly in half. Put the pork belly, pork shoulder, chicken and beef in a cast-iron pot with 125 ml (4 fl oz/½ cup) of water. Put the lid on and put in the oven for 1 hour. Check that nothing is sticking. Reduce the oven to 180°C (350°F/Gas 4) and cook for another 30 minutes.

Wash the beetroot or turnips and cut off the leaves, leaving on a bit of beetroot stem so they don't bleed. Add to the pot with the cabbage slices, carrot, potatoes and sweet potatoes, arranging them beautifully and packing them in tight. Prick the chouriço here and there and put it on top to flavour the dish. Season lightly (the beauty is in the mingling of the different meats and vegetables, so don't overseason) and tuck in the cabbage chunks.

Put the lid back on and return to the oven for 1 hour. Check that nothing is sticking by swaying the pot from side to side. Reduce the oven to 150°C (300°F/Gas 2) and cook for another hour. Remove from the oven but leave the lid on. It will be perfect to eat in an hour or so. Serve with white rice or salad and bread.

(Alternatively, if you are near Furnas on the island of San Miguel, just take your pot full of meat and vegetables to be cooked directly in the earth. If you put it in at around 4 am on Sunday, it will be ready around noon...)
Serves 4–6

Desserts

AND CAKES

MADEIRA CAKE

250 G (9 OZ) *unsalted* BUTTER, *At room temperature* · 225 G (8 OZ/1 CUP) CASTER (*SUPERFINE*) SUGAR ·
1 TEASPOON VANILLA *extract* · 4 EGGS ·
zest and juice of 1 *small* LEMON · 280 G (10 OZ/2¼ CUPS) PLAIN (*ALL-PURPOSE*) FLOUR ·
1½ TEASPOONS BAKING POWDER · 1 TABLESPOON MILK

This is such a lovely plain dense cake that you can serve it with anything — it takes its name for the history that it was traditionally served with a glass of Madeira, and now the island has made it its own. It lasts well, covered, and can just be left for a few days for people to go past and cut off a lean slice. After that you could even toast it and spread with a little jam.

Heat the oven to 170°C (325°F/Gas 3). Butter and flour a 30 x 11 cm (12 x 4 inch) loaf tin.

Whip the butter and sugar together with electric beaters until creamy. Add the vanilla and eggs one at a time, beating well after each one. The mixture may look lumpy for now but will come together fine later.

Whisk in the lemon zest, then the flour and baking powder. Whisk in the lemon juice and milk — it should thin out to a thick batter.

Spoon big dollops of mixture along the length of your tin. You don't need to smooth it out, it will do that as it cooks. Bake for 50–55 minutes or until the cake is golden and crusty and a skewer poked into the middle comes out clean. Cover with foil for the last 15 minutes if it is browning too much.

Loosen the sides with a knife and turn out the cake, then put it back in the tin to cool completely (just to make sure you won't have problems getting it out later). This is a good dense cake that will keep well for several days.

Cuts into about 15 slices

Christmas

BOLO INGLESE

85 G (3 OZ) RAISINS, *chopped* · 85 G (3 OZ) *dried* CRANBERRIES ·
45 G (1½ OZ) CANDIED CHERRIES, *halved* · 45 G (1½ OZ) *mixed* CANDIED FRUIT, *chopped* ·
125 ML (4 FL OZ/½ CUP) WHISKY · 300 G (10½ OZ) CAKE (00) FLOUR ·
1 TEASPOON GROUND CINNAMON · 1½ TEASPOONS BAKING POWDER ·
½ TEASPOON FINE SALT · 250 G (9 OZ) *softened unsalted* BUTTER ·
240 G (8½ OZ) LIGHT BROWN SUGAR · 3 EGGS ·
1 TABLESPOON *clear* HONEY · 50 G (1¾ OZ) WHOLE ALMONDS *WITH SKIN, very roughly chopped*

GLAZE: 60 G (2¼ OZ/⅓ CUP) CASTER (*SUPERFINE*) SUGAR · 2 TABLESPOONS WHISKY

FRUIT FOR ON TOP: *about* 380 G (13½ OZ) *beautiful big chunks of* CANDIED FRUIT (*I used whole
red and green* CHERRIES, ORANGE *rind,* FIGS *and 2 small whole* PEARS)

Look how well dressed this one is. And very Portuguese, despite its name. This recipe is Julio's wife's. She makes it every Christmas in Lisbon and I thank her for adding it to my list of favourite cakes ever. If you don't have exactly the right size loaf tin, use a large ring tin and cook it for 5–10 minutes less. The fruit on top is dramatic large chunks of candied deep red cherries, watermelon, pineapple, melon, cedro… whatever you can get. For a simpler everyday version just leave off the decoration.

Soak the raisins, cranberries, cherries and candied fruit in the whisky for as long as possible while you get ready. Heat your oven to 170°C (325°F/Gas 3). Butter and flour a 30 x 11 x 6 cm (12 x 4 x 2½ inch) loaf tin. (You do need to use this exact size, so all the luscious fruit fits into the cake.) Sift together the flour, cinnamon, baking powder and salt.

Whip the butter and sugar in a large bowl with electric beaters until creamy. Add the eggs one at a time, mixing well after each one. It may seem a bit split, but it will come together well. Add the honey and flour, beating in well to make a thick batter. Stir in the fruit and whisky, sloshing it around so that it all loosens up. Stir in the almonds.

Scrape into the tin. Bake for 1 hour 10 minutes, or until a skewer poked into the centre comes out clean (if it looks like burning around the edges, cover them with foil and leave the middle uncovered). Leave to cool a bit in the tin, then turn out onto a rack.

Meanwhile, prepare the glaze. Stir together the sugar and whisky over low heat without boiling until the sugar has dissolved, then boil until golden and sticky (taking care that it doesn't burn). You can make this in advance and just warm it up on the lowest heat when you're ready to use.

For the top of the cake, use a spoon to dip the base of each fruit piece into the glaze, then arrange the fruit on the cake. Drizzle just a little more glaze here and there (too much on top will set hard and be difficult to eat), sticking the fruit on in big exaggerated chunks. Serve in slices. This is lovely slightly warm but the cake cuts even better the next day and keeps well. You could remove the fruit after cutting a few slices and pack it away for another cake time as this is a real showpiece. You can use as much or as little fruit as you like but I think hyperbole works well here. *Cuts into about 12 slices*

The drive to Furnas is a dream. Something from another land far far away. Up and down winding roads with beautiful cliffs of blue-purple hydrangeas and patchwork green hills, sudden windows of deep navy-blue sea. On the way there are sugar beet, sweet potatoes and syrupy pineapples. Salted red peppers everywhere. There are honey cakes, and people eating 'lapas' straight from the rocks, or later in restaurants grilled with lemon and butter in special nest-like pans.

pudim

COFFEE CREME CARAMELS

CARAMEL: 100 G (3¹/₂ OZ) CASTER (*SUPERFINE*) SUGAR · 1 TABLESPOON PORT OR WHISKY

450 ML (16 FL OZ) MILK · 60 ML (2 FL OZ/¹/₄ CUP) STRONG ESPRESSO COFFEE ·
3 EGGS, *lightly beaten* · 55 G (2 OZ/¹/₄ CUP) CASTER (SUPERFINE) SUGAR ·
· A *few drops of* VANILLA EXTRACT

I loved the way, in Portugal, they would often serve a cinnamon stick in your saucer so that you could slurp your coffee through it like a straw or use it to stir your sugar in. You need to use good strong coffee here so the taste doesn't fade away (I bought a couple of takeaway double espressos from the bar down the road). My lovely Portuguese moulds hold 100 ml (3¹/₂ fl oz) and this mixture is enough to fill eight. If you don't have that size, just use six 125 ml (4 fl oz/¹/₂ cup) moulds, or you could double the whole recipe and use a large ring tin (you'll need to bake it for 1 hour in that case).

To make the caramel, tip the caster sugar into a heavy-based non-stick pan over medium heat and add a tablespoon of water. Heat it up, stirring, until the sugar starts to melt, then tilt the pan to swirl it around — don't stir any more or the sugar will crystallise. Brush down the side of the pan with a wet pastry brush to stop the sugar reforming on the side. Carry on heating and swirling a few times until all the sugar has melted and turned deep golden caramel brown. Stir in the port, watching out for it spitting. Pour into your moulds, swirling so the caramel covers the bottoms. Put the moulds into a large roasting tin and leave to cool while you make the filling. Preheat the oven to 160°C (315°F/ Gas 2–3).

Heat the milk in a saucepan just to boiling point, then whisk in the coffee and remove from the heat. Whisk the eggs, sugar and vanilla together very lightly, just enough to incorporate the sugar but not enough to make it froth. Add a ladleful of the hot milk to the eggs, whipping to acclimatise them, then another ladleful, then pour in all the hot milk and stir together. Pour into the moulds.

Pour boiling water into the roasting tin to come halfway up the sides of the moulds and lift into the oven. Bake for 40 minutes, or until the custard is set.

Leave to cool, then cover with plastic wrap and put in the fridge. These are best eaten the next day when the caramel has dissolved a bit and the custard has firmed up. To turn out, press down with your fingers in gentle dancing piano movements all around the edges of the custards to loosen them from the moulds. Shuffle or shake the mould quite roughly, hold a plate firmly over the top and flip it all over. If the custard refuses to plop down, dip the bottom of the mould in hot water for just a very few seconds. Serve with ever-so-slightly sweetened whipped cream or just plain.

Serves 6–8

On this magical volcanic island people are pulling their cooked food in pots out of the hot earth for Sunday lunch. Among these green greens and blue blues and hot water shooting from the earth between elephant ear-leafed nyams huddled in the warmth, my head is spinning with the quietness of it all. We spend a few hours in the hot spring with everyone going for the cleansing water that streams straight from the belly of the earth. We are healed, and we don't mind our sulphurous swimsuits.

PASSIONFRUIT CREME CARAMEL

CARAMEL: 200 G (7 OZ) CASTER (*SUPERFINE*) SUGAR ·
1 TABLESPOON MARACUJA LIQUEUR *or brandy*

750 ML (26 FL OZ/3 CUPS) MILK · 400 ML (14 FL OZ) TIN CONDENSED MILK ·
7 EGGS, *lightly beaten* · 115 G (4 OZ/½ CUP) CASTER (*SUPERFINE*) SUGAR ·
1 TEASPOON VANILLA EXTRACT · *pulp from 8* PASSIONFRUIT (*about 150 ml/5 fl oz*)

San Miguel in the Azores, with its passionfruit and passionfruit liqueur, has many versions of this pudding. This is a dash lighter than the ones I ate in San Miguel, where less milk and more eggs seemed to be used. You will need an ample high ring tin here, please.

To make the caramel, tip the sugar into a heavy-based non-stick pan over medium heat and add a couple of tablespoons of water. Heat it up, stirring, until the sugar starts to melt, brushing down the side of the pan with a wet pastry brush to stop the sugar reforming on the side. Once the sugar has melted, turn up the heat and stop stirring or it will crystallise. Let it bubble until deep golden brown, tilting the pan if you need to mix it together. Stir in the liqueur (watch for it spitting). Pour into the ring tin, swirling so the caramel covers the bottom. Put the tin in a large roasting tin. Leave to cool while you make the filling.

Preheat your oven to 160°C (315°F/ Gas 2–3). Heat the milk in a saucepan just to boiling point, then whisk in the condensed milk. Whisk the eggs, sugar and vanilla together very lightly — just enough to incorporate the sugar but not enough to make it froth. Add a ladleful of hot milk to the eggs, whipping to acclimatise them, then another ladleful, then pour in all the hot milk and whisk briefly. Stir in the passionfruit pulp.

Pour over the caramel in the tin (if you find it easier, pour it all into a jug and then into the ring tin). The custard will come right to the top. Pour boiling water into the roasting tin to come halfway up the side of the ring tin and lift very carefully into the oven. Bake for 1 hour or until the custard is set.

Leave to cool, then cover with plastic wrap and put in the fridge. This is best eaten the next day when the caramel has dissolved a bit and the custard has firmed up. To turn out, hold a plate firmly over the top of the tin, then flip over quickly, making sure it's landed squarely on the plate before you lift away the tin. Take care not to spill the sauce. *Serves about 8*

RABANADAS
– tipsy slices –

1 LARGE EGG · A *few drops of* VANILLA *extract* · 2 TABLESPOONS CASTER (*SUPERFINE*) SUGAR ·
125 ML (4 FL OZ/½ CUP) MILK · 125 ML (4 FL OZ/½ CUP) CREAM ·
2 X 8 CM (3 INCH) *pieces of yesterday's* BREAD, *sliced horizontally, crusts trimmed*

SYRUP: 1 CM (½ INCH) CINNAMON STICK · 1 *long strip of* ORANGE RIND *and* 1 *of* LEMON RIND ·
2 TABLESPOONS CASTER (*SUPERFINE*) SUGAR · 3 TABLESPOONS RUBY PORT

about 2 TABLESPOONS BUTTER, *for frying* · GROUND CINNAMON, *if you like*

These are traditionally served for Portuguese Christmas, but they're also nice to make on a morning when you wake up early and can't get back to sleep. If you don't have Portuguese bread, use a country-style loaf like ciabatta or baguette. This needs a strong, tight-crumbed bread, not fluffy white cotton-wool slices that will collapse in the soaking.

Whisk the egg, vanilla, sugar, milk and cream in a flat bowl. Add the bread, spoon the liquid over it, and leave to soak for an hour.

To make the syrup, put the cinnamon, orange and lemon rinds, sugar and 185 ml (6 fl oz/¾ cup) of water in a small pan, stir to dissolve the sugar and then bring to the boil. Boil for a few minutes, then add the port. Keep boiling until slightly thickened and syrupy. Remove from the heat.

Heat the butter in a large non-stick frying pan. Shake the bread out of the milky egg and fry until the underside is golden and fraying a bit. Turn and cook until firm and golden. Serve right away, dribbled with some of the syrup and scattered with ground cinnamon. *Serves 2*

cerveja preta

BEER CAKE

175 G (6 OZ) UNSALTED BUTTER, SOFTENED · 175 G (6 OZ/³⁄₄ CUP) CASTER (*SUPERFINE*) SUGAR ·
1 TEASPOON VANILLA EXTRACT · 3 EGGS · 1 TABLESPOON MILK ·
200 ML (7 FL OZ) DARK BEER, *such as a stout* · 1 TEASPOON *finely grated* LEMON ZEST ·
150 ML (5 FL OZ/½ CUP) CLEAR RUNNY HONEY ·
300 G (10½ OZ) CAKE (00) FLOUR · 1 *heaped* TEASPOON BAKING POWDER ·
1 TEASPOON *bicarbonate of* SODA · 1 TEASPOON *ground* CINNAMON · *A good grating of* NUTMEG ·
55 G (2 OZ/½ CUP) CHOPPED WALNUTS (*or any other nuts you like*) ·

This is Lisa from Angola's recipe. Use a lovely dark, full-flavoured beer that will show up well in your cake. I used acacia honey and you can use other nuts instead of walnuts, if you prefer.

Preheat your oven to 180°C (350°F/Gas 4). Butter and flour a large ring tin or a 24 cm (9½ inch) springform tin.

Beat the butter, sugar and vanilla until creamy. Add the eggs one at a time, beating well after each one. Beat in the milk, beer and lemon zest, then whisk in the honey. Sift together the flour, baking powder, soda, cinnamon and nutmeg and stir in. At this point your mixture may look split, but don't worry, it will come together in the baking.

Mix in the nuts and scrape into the tin. Bake for 35–40 minutes (or 10 minutes or so more if you're using a springform tin) until dark golden and a skewer poked into the middle comes out clean. Leave in the tin to cool for 10 minutes before turning out. This is a lovely moist cake that will keep well for many days.

Cuts into about 12 slices

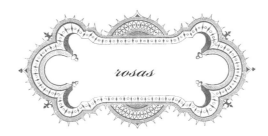

rosas

ROSE CAKE

50 G (1¾ OZ) FRESH YEAST OR 21 G (¾ OZ) DRIED YEAST · 125 ML (4 FL OZ/½ CUP) *warm* MILK ·
115 G (4 OZ/½ CUP) CASTER (*SUPERFINE*) SUGAR, *plus 140 g (5 oz/²/₃ cup) extra* ·
about 550 G (1 LB 4 OZ) PLAIN (*ALL-PURPOSE*) FLOUR · 1 EGG, *plus* 2 YOLKS ·
200 ML (7 FL OZ) CREAM · 150 G (5½ OZ) BUTTER, *softened* · A *pinch of* SALT

This is from Marzia, one of my neighbours in Italy, who got it from someone in Venice, but it is traditionally a Portuguese cake. (It must have fallen off one of the old ships travelling the spice route from Portugal to Venice!) It's often made with some chopped-up candied fruits and other bits and pieces folded in. In Carvoeiro in the Algarve, Ludi and Giovanni came home with a cake very similar to this, which was just one big rose.

Crumble up the fresh yeast (or sprinkle the dried) into a small bowl, add the lukewarm milk and a stolen pinch of the sugar and whisk it together. Leave until the yeast starts to activate and bubble up a bit. Add about a cupful of

flour, or however much it takes to make a soft dough. Knead briefly into a smooth ball, make a cross on top and put it in a large bowl. Cover with a cloth and leave to rise in a warm place for 1½–2 hours until doubled in size or well puffed up.

Whip together the egg, yolks and cream and then add to the risen dough with the 115 g of sugar and the rest of the flour, saving a few spoonfuls for kneading and rolling. Mix well with your fingers to separate any clumps and make it all into a soft smooth dough. Use a heavy-duty mixer for this, if you have one.

Knead the pastry on the largest board you have or just on your work surface (the diameter of this pastry will be 70 cm/28 inches!) Roll out into a circle, dusting your hands with flour to prevent sticking, until about 2 mm ($^1/_{16}$ inch) thick and 70 cm/28 inches across. Butter a 30 cm (12 inch) round non-stick cake tin that is about 6 cm (2$^1/_2$ inches) deep.

Mash up the butter with the extra sugar until soft, creamy and easy to spread. Dab it here and there over the pastry and then gently spread with a butter knife or your hands. Roll up fairly tightly into a long thin sausage.

Cut into 5 cm (2 inch) sections (I got about 15 or 16 roses from my pastry). Stand them upright on your work surface and make about 5 shallow snips around the edge with kitchen scissors. Arrange, standing up, in the tin — one in the middle, some around the outside and a few smaller ones in the middle row. They won't be touching now but space them fairly evenly. They will puff up and join together with that lovely look of flowers in full blossom. Cover and leave in a warm, draught-free place for another 1$^1/_2$–2 hours or so until puffed right up.

Preheat the oven to 180°C (350°F/Gas 4) and bake for about 45 minutes, covering with foil if you think it's browning too much. It's important not to overcook it or it will dry out. Cut into wedges or pull into roses when cooled.

Makes about 15 pieces

I walk down that interesting hilly market road. The immense ocean comes into view on one side and a beautiful exaggerated cartoon hill on the other, speckled with trees and cows and horses that cling casually to its steep slopes. Old people from the mountains in boots and smiling fishermen; I look to the left and want to milk a cow and to the right I feel like diving into the blue. And still I feel that someone has thrown a bucket of silence over me.

breakfast

BOLOS LEVEDOS

— *yeasted milk breads* —

25 G (1 OZ) FRESH YEAST OR 15 G (½ OZ) DRIED YEAST · 250 ML (9 FL OZ/1 CUP) *warm* MILK ·
500 G (1 LB 2 OZ) CAKE (00) FLOUR, *plus a little extra for kneading* ·
150 G (5½ OZ) CASTER (*SUPERFINE*) SUGAR · 2 *pinches of* SALT ·
40 G (1½ OZ) BUTTER, *melted and cooled* · 1 EGG, *lightly whisked*

These we found regularly in the Azores and all loved them. I got the recipe from the lovely old lady at the bakery, but she stopped halfway through and told me I could work the rest out for myself because she suddenly had many customers. I noticed everyone was buying the *bolos levedos* and I asked one of the customers how he liked to eat them. He said, 'Oh, with *marmelada* or butter for breakfast. Some like them even with ham and cheese for a snack,' he continued. You will need a large non-stick frying pan — use the closest thing to a baking stone you can find. I love these: they taste like raw cinnamon bun dough for some reason and the sugar feels elusive, almost like a whisper. You can make the dough into one large cake

and cut into wedges to serve. They don't keep very well, so either eat them straightaway or freeze them in plastic bags.

Crumble up the fresh yeast (or sprinkle in the dried) into a small bowl, add the luke-warm milk, a handful of the flour and a stolen pinch of the sugar and whisk it all together. Leave until the yeast starts to activate and bubble up a bit. Meanwhile, put the rest of the flour, sugar and salt in a large bowl and make a well in it.

Pour the foamy yeast mixture into the well with the melted butter and egg, mixing in well with a wooden spoon until you have a soft rough sticky ball. Sprinkle some of the extra flour onto your work surface and, with floured hands, gently knead for a minute or so until the ball is smoothish. (This is a gentle bringing together of the dough without much flour or force.) Put into a large bowl, cover with a tea towel and leave for 2–3 hours in a warm place until it has puffed up well. Line a large baking tray with baking paper.

Divide the dough into about 12 portions, roll them gently into a ball with your palms and a little of the flour and put them on the trays, leaving a little space inbetween. Cover loosely with another sheet of baking paper and a cloth on top of that. Leave to rise for another hour.

Heat up a large heavy-based frying pan or stone to hot then reduce the heat to low. Take each ball of dough (working with four or so at a time depending on the size of your pan). Flatten each ball as smoothly as you can without knocking the air out too much to make a flat disk about 10 cm (4 inches) wide. Dust a little flour on both sides and put into the hot pan over gentle heat. Turn over carefully when the undersides are deep golden (remember they need to have cooked halfway through if they're not to have doughy centres). Cook until the new underside is deep golden and remove to a cloth-lined basket while you cook the others. Cut a cooled one open to check it's cooked.

These are good both warm and cold. Left out they tend to harden and don't keep well, but are great toasted and spread with butter and jam. *Makes 12*

Today I came out onto the balcony very early as it is our last day in San Miguel. It was just at that lovely time of day when the sun was lighting up the first shadows on the trees. Some distant shouts from the few fishermen dotted here and there on the Atlantic, and soft waves rolling up onto the dark volcanic shores... I am in paradise, trying to decide the colour of this ocean: navy, grey, silver, powder, ice? It is changing all the time... just as I decide. Azores, I think is its colour.

I will be back.

SUSPIROS

— sighs —

4 EGG WHITES, *at room temperature* · A *good pinch of* SALT ·
225 G (8 OZ/1 CUP) CASTER (*SUPERFINE*) SUGAR · A *few drops of* VANILLA EXTRACT

Meringues are everywhere in Portugal, in the windows of all the pastry shops. You can serve them plain, just for a sugar rush, or crush them over a dessert. You can also fold a couple of tablespoons of chopped walnuts into them before baking. Use the egg yolks for making *pastéis de nata*.

These are just meringues, but what a name — *suspiros* are 'sighs' and that is how they look and sound when you bite them. It is easy to imagine the lovely Portuguese housewife in her apron leaning against her kitchen bench and exhaling a deep breath (of appreciation?) at the sight of these light and airy clouds.

Preheat your oven to 100°C (200°F/Gas ½) and line two trays with baking paper. Beat the egg whites and salt into very firm peaks with electric beaters in a spotless metal bowl. Beat in the sugar, in small batches, until the mixture is bright white and so stiff it's almost climbing up the beaters. Beat in the vanilla and spoon into a large piping bag fitted with a fluted nozzle.

Pipe smallish meringues (I made them small — just one squeeze of my big orange piping bag), leaving a bit of space between them for puffing up. Bake for about 1 hour until firm and crisp. Turn the oven off and leave the meringues inside with the door ajar so they cool down slowly. When completely cold, store in an airtight container. *Makes about 40*

sighs plus

DATES, FIGS, ALMONDS AND SIGHS

185 ML (6 FL OZ/¾ CUP) CREAM · 20 G (¾ OZ) BUTTER · 4 FRESH DATES, *halved, stones removed* ·
4 OR 5 *plump dried* FIGS, *halved* · 1 TABLESPOON SOFT BROWN SUGAR ·
3 TABLESPOONS BRANDY · *about* 16 WHOLE ALMONDS *with skin, roughly chopped* ·
GROUND CINNAMON · 2–3 *small* MERINGUES *per person*

This was inspired by the *suspiros* (meringues) and bag of beautiful almonds we brought back from the Algarve. This has dates and figs served in layers with whipped cream and cinnamon, like a very rough Portuguese trifle. It is about right for two people, so change it as needs be for as many as you're feeding.

Whip the cream into soft peaks that will just hold up on a plate. Melt the butter in a small saucepan with the dates, figs and brown sugar and, when it starts to sizzle, add the brandy.

Cook until gooey and just starting to crisp, but still with some sauce. Leave to cool a little.

Toast the nuts in a small dry frying pan until a bit golden, taking care not to burn them. Leave to cool.

Spoon some of the dates and figs onto a plate and top with a generous blob of cream, another spoonful of dates, figs and sauce, a scattering of nuts, a sprinkling of cinnamon and a couple of whole or crushed meringues on top. *Serves 2*

Belém

PASTEIS DE NATA

— Portuguese tarts —

PASTRY: 250 G (9 OZ) *cold unsalted* BUTTER, *chopped* · 250 G (9 OZ) CAKE (00) FLOUR ·
40 G (1½ OZ) CASTER (*SUPERFINE*) SUGAR · A *pinch of* SALT

CUSTARD FILLING: 100 G (3½ OZ) CASTER (*SUPERFINE*) SUGAR · 30 G (1 OZ) CAKE (00) FLOUR ·
185 ML (6 FL OZ/¾ CUP) MILK · ½ TEASPOON VANILLA EXTRACT ·
1 *strip of* LEMON RIND · 3 EGG YOLKS · 125 ML (4 FL OZ/½ CUP) CREAM

I came back from Portugal with special *pastéis* tins in my enthusiasm for making these. My tins are 7 cm across the top, 3.5 cm high and slope down to 4 cm across the base. And they're all individual, not in a tray. You can use anything with a similar measure, such as muffin tins, or, better still, patty pan tins which are a bit lower. Save the egg whites from here to make *suspiros*. I have seen a few different ways of making these… they are not the easiest at first go, but once you've tried them you'll see they are worth it. You need a good hot oven, or yours might need longer to get those dark golden gorgeous blotches here and there.

To make the pastry, mix the butter in a bowl with the flour, sugar and salt until crumbly looking (rather like damp sand). Pour in 3 tablespoons of water (and a dribble more if you think it needs it) and mix until it comes together. (Alternatively, pulse together in a food processor.) Press the dough into a ball, flatten a bit and wrap in plastic. Put in the fridge for a couple of hours (you can make this a day in advance, or even freeze it at this stage).

Roll out the dough on a lightly floured surface to make a 40 x 35 cm (16 x 14 inch) rectangle. Cut in half lengthways and roll up each rectangle along its length to give two long sausages. Trim away the rough ends.

Cut each sausage into about six lengths of 6 cm (2½ inches). Stand each one upright like a cylinder and then press down into the cylinder with both your thumbs to make a flower shape. Cup it with your hands and swivel around, pressing gently with your thumbs and forefingers to make a cosy nest as you spin. Don't squash the pastry too much — it needs to flake and puff up nicely when it cooks.

Fit the pastry into your tins (see introduction), pressing down so it takes the shape and the pastry extends a little above the edge. Make sure the bases are thin — push the pastry out a bit more and smooth the top edges, rolling over and pressing again to neaten into nice nests. If the weather is hot, you may have to refrigerate them again for a while to work the pastry along. Put them back in the fridge while you make the custard.

To make the custard, put the sugar in a small heavy-based pan with 3 tablespoons of water. Stir over heat to dissolve the sugar and then let it come to a gentle boil. Cook until thickened a bit but not about to caramelise.

Meanwhile, put the flour in a wide bowl with a little of the milk, whisking to make a smooth slurry. Heat the rest of the milk in a small heavy-based pan with the vanilla and lemon rind. As the milk is about to come to the boil, add it to the flour slurry. Remove the lemon rind and whisk immediately until smooth. Whisk in the egg yolks and then tip it all back into the pan, whisking for a minute or two over low heat until it is smooth and the eggs have heated a little.

When your sugar syrup is ready, pour in a slow steady drizzle into the hot milk mixture, whisking continuously. Remove from the heat and mix in the cream, then pour into a jug (just to make filling the pastries easier). Heat your oven to 220°C (425°F/Gas 7).

Take the pastries out of the fridge and fill them two-thirds full of custard (you should have exactly the right amount of custard for twelve). Bake for 15–20 minutes, depending on your oven, or until you can see the pastry is cooked and golden and the custards have a couple of dark amber speckles. You can remove any that look ready, leaving the paler ones for longer if necessary.

Once they're all out of the oven, leave them in the tins but swivel them around a bit so they don't stick while cooling. Serve at room temperature, plain, or as they serve them in the pastry shops of Belém: with a sachet of cinnamon, a sachet of icing sugar and a sashay out of the door... *Makes 12*

STA
ZITA

– *In the pastelaria de Belém* –

I arrive by tram, passing the lovely pale yellows, pinks and whites of Lisbon. To Belém and the very tower where so many caravels set off centuries ago. And then to the *pastelaria*. You can watch through glass doors while the *pastéis* are made. I sit down and drink a milky coffee and try to absorb the wonder of it all among so many blue and white tiles. The pastry is so thin and crisp in layers. Their shape is beautiful and their imperfections lovely (in fact, I am thrilled that the Portuguese can get away with serving something that is almost burnt in places, and to such applause). Two or three women stretch the puffed rounds of dough with skill into longer thinner buttery-looking ropes. Another, at lightning speed, cuts them into perfect short lengths, and then another presses them into the thousand-times-used tins in their hundreds of trays. Yet another squeezes the exact amount of cream into each pastry case and then, whoosh, into the furnace they go and come out looking the beauties they are. And all this going on among the tangle of people, waiters threading their way through them, and the labyrinth of rooms and *pastéis*. Coffees are rushed past on faded silvery trays and the atmosphere falls somewhere between canteen and palace. The pastries leave the shop in lovely long blue-and-white boxes almost as fast as they come out of the oven.
And off I go, very pleased, to witness for myself the masterpiece of turned layers of manueline ropes in the Mosteiro dos Jerónimos almost next door, and the extremely high ceilings, and the absolute 'how did they make all this?'
Aren't humans amazing? Between the layers of the *pastéis* and the layers of this building, how on earth did they do this?

PINEAPPLE CAKE

350 G (12 OZ/1½ CUPS) CASTER (*SUPERFINE*) SUGAR •
1 *fresh* PINEAPPLE *of about 650 g* (*1½ lb*) • 4 EGGS, *separated* •
200 G (7 OZ) *unsalted* BUTTER • 200 G (7 OZ) CAKE (00) FLOUR • 1 TEASPOON BAKING POWDER

This is a very popular cake in Portugal and is lovely for breakfast, afternoon tea or as an anytime snack. I had this very often on the island of San Miguel, made with their lovely pineapples. If you can't get a fresh pineapple then tinned will do, and this is also beautiful made with apple slices. You can also bake it in a high ring tin if that's what you have in your cupboard. In Portugal it's very often made that way.

Heat your oven to 180°C (350°F/Gas 4) and grease a 30 x 11 cm (12 x 4 inch) loaf tin. Flour the tin very lightly, then rap on your work surface to remove any excess.

To make the caramel, tip 115 g (4 oz/ ½ cup) of the caster sugar into a heavy-based non-stick pan over medium heat and add a couple of teaspoons of water. Heat it up until the sugar starts to melt, then tilt the pan to swirl it around — don't stir or the sugar will crystallise. Carry on heating and swirling a few times until all the sugar has melted and turned golden caramel brown; watch carefully, it can burn in a few seconds. Pour carefully into the tin, tilting so the caramel covers the bottom. Leave to cool.

Peel your pineapple and cut out any eyes. Cut into 1 cm (½ inch) rings, then twizzle out the core and eat or discard it. You will need about ten nice rings. Arrange the rings over the base of the tin, overlapping them as much as possible. (Try to imagine how it will look when you turn it upside down to serve.)

Whip the egg whites into soft peaks. Cream together the butter and the remaining sugar. Add the egg yolks, beating them in well, then sift in the flour and baking powder. Fold in the egg whites.

Spoon into the tin, over and around the pineapple, tapping the tin on the work surface to settle it in.

Bake for about 55 minutes to 1 hour, until the top is puffed and beautifully golden and a skewer comes out fairly clean when poked into the middle (this will still be quite a moist cake). Cool for a while, then loosen the sides with a knife and turn out. Cut into thick slices to serve, either warm or completely cooled.

Cuts into about 12 slices

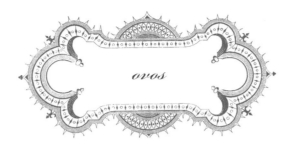

ovos

SERICAIA

— Portuguese egg pudding —

250 ML (9 FL OZ/1 CUP) MILK ⋅ A *small* CINNAMON STICK ⋅
4 EGGS, *separated* ⋅ 4 TABLESPOONS CASTER (*SUPERFINE*) SUGAR ⋅
1 TEASPOON VANILLA EXTRACT ⋅ 4 TABLESPOONS PLAIN (*ALL-PURPOSE*) FLOUR ⋅
grated zest of 1 LEMON ⋅ 2 TEASPOONS *ground* CINNAMON

We ate this in Alentejo, with their beautiful Elvas sugarplums in syrup (overleaf). It's a light egg pudding, a bit like clafoutis or a cinnamon omelette almost, and is usually baked in a large round terracotta dish.

Heat your oven to 180°C (350°F/Gas 4). Butter and flour a 26 cm (10¹/₂ inch) round dish that's about 4 cm (1¹/₂ inches) deep (not springform or the mixture will leak out).

Heat the milk and cinnamon stick in a pan on the stovetop until it's coming to the boil. Whip the egg whites with electric beaters until creamy but not too stiff. Set on one side and work quickly.

Whip the egg yolks, sugar and vanilla with the beaters until creamy, then beat in the flour and lemon zest until thick and well combined. With the motor running, strain the very hot milk over the mixture and beat until smooth and creamy.

Fold in the fluffy whites, working and folding with a whisk until they are completely incorporated but not flattened and losing their volume.

Pour into your dish and sprinkle the top generously with cinnamon. You can make shapes with the cinnamon, flowers or stripes, or just sprinkle it all over in an even layer.

Bake for 20–25 minutes until the top is well puffed and firm, even cracked in a couple of places. Leave to cool and settle, then carefully transfer to a serving plate or just cut into wedges straight from the dish. Eat on the same day. *Serves 6*

nuns & plums

PLUMS IN SYRUP

400 G (14 OZ) RED PLUMS · 200 G (7 OZ) ELVAS PLUMS ·
3 TABLESPOONS CASTER (*SUPERFINE*) SUGAR · 1 TABLESPOON HONEY ·
2 TABLESPOONS PORT · 20 G (³/₄ OZ) *unsalted* BUTTER ·
2 TEASPOONS *grated* LEMON ZEST · 1 *piece of* CINNAMON STICK

I have made a mix here of red plums and Elvas sugarplums. I came home with a beautiful wooden box holding eight of these preserved sugared greengages, and they look almost like prunes, small, semi-dried but still succulent. The *ameixas d'Elvas* have been made since the middle ages and were traditionally candied by the nuns of the town. If you can't find Elvas plums (or nuns to make them for you!), then make up the weight with a couple of extra red plums, or you could even add some figs or other fruit.

Halve your red plums and take out the stones. Put them, cut side up, in a single layer in a baking dish where they fit snugly, with the whole Elvas plums scattered around, if you're using them. Sprinkle with the sugar and drizzle with the honey, port and 3 tablespoons of water. Dot a blob of butter over each plum. (You can get this far, then cover and keep the plums on one side for a few hours before baking.)

Heat the oven to 200°C (400°F/Gas 6). Bake the plums, uncovered, for 15–20 minutes until they are nicely roasted but not falling apart. The juice should have collected around them and be bubbling up.

Serve hot or at room temperature with a wedge of *sericaia* and some syrup drizzled over the top. Scatter with a little extra cinnamon if you like. *Serves 4–6*

Maria Alice

TEA CAKES

85 G (3 OZ) BUTTER, *softened* · 4 TABLESPOONS CASTER (*SUPERFINE*) SUGAR ·
A *few drops of* VANILLA EXTRACT · 2 EGGS ·
4 TABLESPOONS PLAIN (*ALL-PURPOSE*) FLOUR · ½ TEASPOON BAKING POWDER ·
candied ORANGE OR LEMON *zest*, PINE NUTS, *chopped* WALNUTS OR SOUR CHERRIES, *as you like*

These are Daniela's mum's tea cakes and they have an outfit for every occasion. You might like to decorate the tops before cooking, with a few chopped up bits of almonds with their skins on or a small slice of dried fig, or simply sprinkle with some decorative sugar. For special occasions decorate the cooked cakes with thinly rolled out marzipan rounds, cut to fit and stuck on with a blob of cherry or quince jam. To change the flavour of the batter replace the vanilla with a teaspoon of ground cinnamon or 2 teaspoons of grated citrus zest.

Heat your oven to 180°C (350°F/Gas 4). Have a large baking tray ready, lined with about 45 tiny paper cups. Cream the butter, sugar and vanilla until smooth. Whisk in the eggs, one at a time, beating well after each one. Add the flour and baking powder and mix until smooth.

Fill each paper cup about half-full (the cakes will rise). If you feel like adding something extra, push into the mixture a few small bits of candied orange or lemon zest, a few nuts or half a sour cherry (that you've patted dry with kitchen paper first).

Bake for about 15 minutes until golden and puffed up. Leave to cool, then keep in a tin. These are good for tea or breakfast, or to just pop in your mouth as you go past the tin.
Makes about 45

QUINCE MARMALADE

about 2 KG (4 LB 8 OZ) QUINCES · THE *juice of* 1 LEMON · *about* 1.8 KG (4 LB) SUGAR

This is often served for breakfast and is lovely with bread and one of the incredibly creamy Portuguese cheeses such as *Serra da Estrela*. On one restaurant menu I saw a combination of cheese and quince paste called 'Romeo and Julietta', which I thought sounded lovely.

This makes A LARGE AMOUNT. But my feeling is, once you've got hold of your so-rare and special quinces and stirred the pot until your arm hurts, you might as well make a big big batch and send some round to your friends. It will keep for quite a while in an airtight container in the fridge or you could just make half or quarter of the amount and choose a suitable mould or tin.

Wash the quinces and cut them up, skin and pips and all. Put them in a large heavy-based pan, add about 1.25 litres (44 fl oz/5 cups) of water and the lemon juice and bring to the boil. Lower the heat a dash, cover the pan and simmer for an hour or so, stirring often, until the quinces are soft and turning rosy coloured.

Cool a little, then pass through the fine holes of a food mill, discarding the bits that insist they won't go through.

Weigh your quince — I had about 2.25 kg (5 lb). For every kilo, you should use about 800 g (1 lb 12 oz) sugar. Weigh out your sugar and put the quinces and sugar back in the pan. Bring to a gentle boil (I use a simmer mat so nothing sticks), stirring continuously so nothing can stick and burn.

Lower the heat and simmer for 2 1/2–3 hours, stirring very often, until it is thick, with a beautiful deep colour and falls onto itself when you drop a spoonful from a height, rather than vanishing into nothing. It should start to pull away from the side of the pan when you turn it with a wooden spoon. At the end you might need to stir constantly to prevent sticking and burning.

Very lightly oil a very large (3 litres/ 105 fl oz/12 cup) ring tin with corn oil (I wipe it with kitchen paper so it's not too oily.) Pour your jam into the tin and flatten the top with your wooden spoon. Leave to cool, covering with a net or sheet of greaseproof paper so that no moisture can form. Leave overnight so it dries out a bit (if you have an oven with a pilot light that you can leave on that's a perfect place for drying it out). Turn out onto a plate (you might have to dip the tin briefly in hot water to release it). Store in an airtight container in the fridge, or cut up into slabs, wrap in plastic and keep in the fridge. *Makes an enormous amount*

Azores

CARAMEL CAKE

200 G (7 OZ) CASTER (*SUPERFINE*) SUGAR · 125 ML (4 FL OZ/½ CUP) CREAM ·
125 ML (4 FL OZ/½ CUP) MILK · 200 G (7 OZ) *unsalted* BUTTER, *softened* ·
3 EGGS · 1 TEASPOON VANILLA EXTRACT ·
250 G (9 OZ/2 CUPS) PLAIN (*ALL-PURPOSE*) FLOUR · 1½ TEASPOONS BAKING POWDER

This has a lovely lingering taste of caramel and is best when it's a bit damp still inside, so judge the strength of your own oven so that it doesn't dry out. This would be lovely with mangoes or pineapple and perhaps whipped cream and raspberries.

Preheat your oven to 180°C (350°F/Gas 4). Butter and flour a 24 cm (9½ inch) spring-form tin. Put the sugar in a pan over medium heat and let it melt slowly and turn to caramel. Don't stir the sugar, just tilt the pan often so that it melts evenly and turns a deep golden caramel. Remove from the heat and carefully whisk in the combined cream and milk, standing back as it will splash up. Whisk until

it is all added. If the caramel hardens and forms solid bits, whisk it over very low heat to dissolve them, then remove and let it cool a bit.

Whip the butter briefly in a large bowl until creamy. Pour in the caramel and whisk together well (the heat remaining in the caramel will melt the butter), then beat in the eggs, one by one, and the vanilla. It will be a lovely sloppy mixture – thinner than your usual cake mixture – so carry on beating until it thickens a bit. Whisk in the sifted flour and baking powder until it's all thick and creamy.

Scrape into the tin and bake for about 35–40 minutes until firm and crusty golden on top but still moist inside. Cool before removing from the tin. *Cuts into about 12 slices*

João

HONEY TART

500 G (1 LB 2 OZ) *clear runny* HONEY · 200 G (7 OZ) BUTTER, *at room temperature* ·
250 ML (9 FL OZ/1 CUP) MILK · 300 G (10½ OZ) CAKE (00) FLOUR

This is just like eating honey. The honey you use here is exactly the taste you'll end up with. I used acacia, which is very mild, but the honey pot in the restaurant where I had this was clover: '*flor predominante trevo*'. The recipe is from João who served it to me at The Alcide. I loved it so much that I stood outside the restaurant for an hour, waiting to ask how it was made. Finally he came out and wrote it down and I felt as if I had struck gold.

Heat the oven to 180°C (350°F/Gas 4). Butter two 20 cm (8 inch) springform cake tins.

Put the honey into a mixer or somewhere you'll be able to mix it with a hand-held blender. Add the butter and a bit of the milk slowly and purée. Add the rest of the milk and then the flour, and slowly and quickly purée so it is well mixed but not gluey. Pour into the tins and bake for 35–40 minutes, until the tarts are nicely browned and have left the sides of the tins. Slice when cool. *Makes about 24 small rich slices*

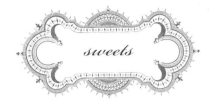

CHURROS

50 G (1¾ OZ) *unsalted* BUTTER · 90 G (3 OZ/¾ CUP) PLAIN (*ALL-PURPOSE*) FLOUR ·
1½ TABLESPOONS CASTER (*SUPERFINE*) SUGAR · ¼ TEASPOON BAKING POWDER ·
A pinch of SALT · 1½ EGGS · OIL, *for frying* ·
ICING (*CONFECTIONER'S*) SUGAR *and* CINNAMON, *to serve*

This is Rachele's, who I met in Lisbon, but we ate these in the north of Portugal at the funfair... everyone on the streets eating sugar-dusted churros from paper packets.

Perhaps these are more Spanish than Portuguese, but you know how it is with your neighbours... you peep over the fence, are inspired by their flowers, and have all the same ingredients and climate so everything grows the same. I think countries are just the same, peeping over borders and being inspired by what they find.

You'll need a piping bag or syringe with a 1 cm (½ inch) star-shaped nozzle to give these their lovely crisp ridges.

Put 150 ml (5 fl oz) of water and the butter in a small heavy-based pan and heat until the butter has melted, then bring just to a boil. Meanwhile, mix together the flour, sugar, baking powder and salt. Whisk the eggs. When the water comes to the boil, remove it from the heat, pour in the flour mixture and stir vigorously with a wooden spoon until you have a soft pastry with no lumps. Return to the heat for a minute or two until the mixture forms a smooth ball. Tip the dough into a bowl and leave to cool a bit.

Using electric beaters, beat in the egg bit by bit until it is completely incorporated and the dough is smooth and glossy. Put into your pastry bag with a 1 cm (½ inch) star nozzle.

Heat enough oil to cover the base of your frying pan. Squeeze 10–12 cm (4 inch) lengths of dough directly into the hot oil, nipping off the ends cleanly with scissors or a sharp knife. Fry on both sides, turning when crisp and golden, and lift out onto kitchen paper to absorb the oil. Serve, sprinkled very generously with icing sugar and cinnamon. *Makes about 10*

melão

MELON SORBET WITH PORT

1 _lovely ripe green sweet_ MELON (ABOUT 1.3 KG/3 LB) • 85 G (3 OZ/⅓ CUP) CASTER (_SUPERFINE_) SUGAR • 1 TABLESPOON LEMON JUICE • _glasses of_ RUBY PORT, _to serve_

I love this for its colours. I tasted some of the best melons I have ever had during my summer in Portugal. The amount of sugar you need will depend on the sweetness of the melon you start with. If you don't have an ice cream machine you can turn this sorbet into a granita: spread the puréed mixture into a shallow tray and put in the freezer, then stir every 2 hours with a fork to break up the ice crystals as they form. Repeat two or three times. The granita is ready when it's almost set but still grainy.

Halve the melon and scoop out the seeds, saving the juice in a bowl as you go. Scoop out the melon flesh into the bowl, sprinkle with the sugar and mash up roughly with a potato masher. Leave to mingle for a bit so the sugar melts, then purée until smooth. Pour into a shallow tray, cover and put in the fridge until completely cold. Transfer to your ice cream machine and churn, following the manufacturer's instructions.

Add the lemon juice when the sorbet is almost churned. Scoop into bowls and serve with glasses of port, to drizzle over the top or drink alongside. _Serves 6_

ruby

PORT ICE CREAM

170 ML (5½ FL OZ/⅔ CUP) RUBY PORT · 85 G (3 OZ/⅓ CUP) CASTER (*SUPERFINE*) SUGAR · 310 ML (11 FL OZ/1¼ CUPS) THICK CREAM · 310 ML (11 FL OZ/1¼ CUPS) MILK

Driving back from Porto I stopped in Guimaraes. I had been eyeing it on the map, curious to see the *pousada* in the old convent. The friendly man in the central *pousada* ran his pen unhurriedly along the map to show me, but I still managed to get lost and had to ask a policeman for help. 'Just a moment please, I will get you an escort,' he said, and had a colleague drive his motorbike ten minutes up the road just to satisfy a whim of mine. The people of Portugal are like their sea, I found — beautiful, calm, spacious and unsuspicious.

You can use more port here if you like a strong 'porty' flavour. I just love the antique-rose colour of this ice cream.

Put the port in a pan over low heat, add the sugar and stir until dissolved. Leave to cool. Whisk the cream gently, then add the milk and drizzle in the sugared port. Mix together well.

Pour into a shallow tray, cover and put in the fridge until completely cold. Transfer to your ice cream machine and churn, following the manufacturer's instructions. Scoop into serving glasses and serve with a biscuit or two and perhaps some fruit — fresh figs or cooked plums are lovely. *Serves 4–6*

gelado

CITRUS, BAY LEAF AND CINNAMON ICE CREAM WITH GINJINHA

3 EGGS · 115 G (4 OZ/¹/₂ CUP) CASTER (*SUPERFINE*) SUGAR · ¹/₂ TEASPOON VANILLA EXTRACT ·
375 ML (13 FL OZ/1¹/₂ CUPS) MILK · 375 ML (13 FL OZ/1¹/₂ CUPS) THICK CREAM ·
4 CM (*about 2 inch*) CINNAMON STICK · 1 *long strip of* ORANGE RIND *and* 1 OF LEMON RIND ·
2 *FRESH* BAY LEAVES, *torn in half* · GINJINHA (*overleaf*), *to serve*

I made this ice cream especially to go with the beautiful *ginjinha*.

Whisk the eggs, sugar and vanilla in a largish bowl until thickened. Slowly heat the milk, cream, cinnamon, orange and lemon rind and bay leaves in a heavy-based pan. Heat it up slowly, so the flavours have a chance to infuse. When it comes to a rolling boil, add a ladleful to the eggs, beating well to acclimatise them. Beat in another ladleful, then add it all and mix well. Pour it all back into the pan and place over the lowest possible heat. Cook, whisking constantly, until slightly thickened.

Remove from the heat and whisk now and then while it cools. Leave all the bits in the custard. Pour into a shallow tray, cover and put in the fridge until completely cold. Sieve, transfer to your ice cream machine and churn, following the manufacturer's instructions.

Serve with some *ginjinha* and a couple of the cherries dribbled over the top, or any other liqueur you like. *Serves 4–6*

sour cherries

LICOR DE GINJA (GINJINHA)

500 G (1 LB 2 OZ) SOUR CHERRIES · 220 G (7½ OZ/1 CUP) SUGAR ·
1 _small_ CINNAMON STICK, _halved_ · 1 _large strip of_ LEMON RIND ·
1 LITRE (35 FL OZ/4 CUPS) AGUARDENTE _or brandy_

Tiny glasses of this, with a couple of cherries in them, are served out of beautiful little cubby holes in the Lisbon streets at any time of day or night. Sour cherries are only available for such a short season, so if you buy them in the spring and make this, you can have your cherries again at Christmastime. Aguardente is a popular Portuguese sugar-based spirit. One book I've read says to leave this for at least a year for the flavours to infuse, but even six months is good.

For this you need a 1.5 litre (52 fl oz/6 cup) glass bottle with an opening large enough to pop in the cherries. Take extra care sterilising the bottle first as you'll be keeping this for a while. Wash the bottle thoroughly (a hot dish-washer is perfect), then pour boiling water into the clean bottle and leave it up-ended on a clean towel or in a warm oven until dry.

Remove the stalks from the cherries and then wash them under cold water, drain and pat dry on a clean towel. Take out the stones (a cherry-pipper makes this an easy job).

Put the cherries in the bottle and top with the sugar, cinnamon stick and lemon rind, using a funnel if necessary. Pour in the aguardente. The cherries need to be covered completely and the bottle containing as little air in the top as possible, so use more or less.

Seal the bottle and store in a cool dark place for the flavours to infuse. Shake the bottle daily for the first few days to make sure all the sugar has dissolved. You need to leave this for a couple of months to mature before you start drinking it, but the longer you can leave it the better the flavour will be. Lovely dribbled over ice cream. _Makes 1.5 litres (52 fl oz/6 cups)_

- *A last evening in Lisbon* -

We walk down the beautiful pavements. It's easy to move smoothly, I feel, in Lisbon. I find it calm and together — there and yet not quite there. We go to the bar at the Alentejo House restaurant and order grilled chouriço and a bacalhau and chickpea salad. There are nice square chips coming out of the kitchen, like the ones we had on top of the pork and clams.

Later, we set off down our back road and past that tiny yellow tram — off to the *ginjeria* where there is a helluva queue. I notice, it being Saturday, that they are serving in small paper cups. When I ask the man, he says, glasses by day and paper by night. Of course, I did prefer the glass but now we can walk with our cups and I notice around me how many people are doing the same, then picking out the sour cherries to eat. There is a lovely atmosphere on the street. I love Lisbon more and more each day.

We leave by taxi then. With its old–leather smell, it hums its way past the fading *azulejos* and sneaked views of the water that come up now and then, like a trick, a small side show. At the airport there are many people shouting in various Portuguese colours and dialects…

ACKNOWLEDGEMENTS

Piri piri∗ starfish

THIS IS MY CHANCE TO THANK THE VERY MANY WHO
BROUGHT THIS BOOK TO LIFE.

Thank you Daniela de Jesus for sharing your invaluable family recipes, and your time
and enthusiasm with me. I thank your mother, Maria Alice, too.
To Richard Pflederer for your historical expertise and advice. Thank you also to your
family, Sue and Lisa, for your help and encouragement.
To all of you who helped so graciously with the recipes... Thank you *truly* Corinne,
Tina, Peta, Melissa, Natasha and your aunt Helen, Artemis E, Manny, Stephen,
Julia, Jem, Marzia, Mariella, Rita, Andrea, Barbara and Diana, Ines, Teresa, João,
Philippe, Julio and your wife, Rachele, Pedro and Marco and all at The Hotel
Britania in Lisbon, Washington, Carla Fontes, Eduardo Melo, Albertina, Carlo,
Daniela Machado, Inca, Artemis H, Mario and Wilma, and Adam. Thanks to
José Pedroso from the lovely Lisbon antique shop, 'a Idade do Armàrio'.
Thank you Luisa for all your very generous help.
To Kay and Juliet, thank you for the marvellous ticket to travel.
To Michelle, for your precision and generosity. To Jane for julienning all
the words just right. And to all at Murdoch, *especially* Gayna.
As ever, a humble thank-you to my family Giovanni, Yasmine and Cassia,
and to mom, dad, Nin and Ludi.

To Portugal for having been so kind without realising it. And to my team...
Michail, Manos and Lisa — I thank you for your beautiful eyes and souls.

Tess x

Inspiration cookbook authors: Mimi Jardin, Ana Patuleia Ortins, Carol Robertson, Antonio Silva, Balbina Pereira
Inspiration authors: José Saramago, Fernando Pessoa, Eça de Queiroz, Martin Page, CR Boxer, Denis Guedj
Inspiration music: Amalia Rodriguez, Mariza, Katia Guerreiro, Cesaria Evora, Madredeus, Dulce Pontes